D0934373

Conflict in Ukraine

Conflict in Ukraine

The Unwinding of the Post–Cold War Order

Rajan Menon and Eugene Rumer

A Boston Review Book
The MIT Press
Cambridge, Massachusetts
London, England

© 2015 Massachusetts Institute of Technology

All rights reserved. No part of this book may be reproduced in any form by any electronic or mechanical means (including photocopying, recording, or information storage and retrieval) without permission in writing from the publisher.

MIT Press books may be purchased at special quantity discounts for business or sales promotional use. For information, please email special_sales@mitpress.mit.edu.

This book was set in Stone by *Boston Review* and printed and bound in the United States of America.

Library of Congress Cataloging-in-Publication Data is available.
ISBN 978-0-262-02904-9 (hc. : alk paper)

10   9   8   7   6   5   4   3   2   1

To Roger E. Kanet and Oles M. Smolansky (R.M.)

and

To the memory of Stephen M. Meyer (E.R.)

Contents

Introduction: Ukraine 2014

"Crisis" is an overused word, one that has been cheapened as a result. Yet it aptly describes the train of events that followed Ukrainian President Viktor Yanukovych's decision in November 2013 to back away from Ukraine's Association Agreement (AA) with the European Union. (Ukraine and the EU had begun negotiations on the AA in March 2007; it was initialed, but not signed, in February 2012.[1]) Yanukovych's choice proved fateful, for the AA was no ordinary document. It was a symbol of hope for those Ukrainians (well represented in the country's central and western regions) who dreamed of integrating with Europe, but not for those (chiefly in the south and east) who favored retaining close ties with Russia.

Soon, protestors swarmed Kyiv's streets. Blood was shed following Yanukovych's decision to unleash riot police and snipers to quell the rebellion. This violence merely enraged and enlarged the crowds. By February, with the death toll mounting and his political position perilous, Yanukovych opted for the olive branch. On the 21st, with EU emissaries mediating, he signed a pact with the leaders of the revolt.[2] Its provisions included forming a "national unity" government within ten days, pruning presidential powers, restoring the 2004 constitution, and organizing early elections, under new guidelines, by year's end. American and European leaders praised the compromise, and so did Russia, but it failed to stick on the street, and figures in the opposition bent on ousting Yanukovych rejected it. Any solution involving him became impossible. Having already lost the support of the parliament (Verkhovna Rada), he fled the following day, Feburary 22.

Yanukovych's ouster merely moved the crisis to a new, more dangerous phase. What many Ukrainians, along with Western governments, hailed as a revolution against a corrupt, authoritarian regime, Russia denounced as an "extra-constitutional coup" against an elected leader.

Things soon took a turn for the worse. With Yanukovych out of the picture, the leaders of Crimea, Ukraine's sole Russian-majority province, organized a referendum on secession on March 16—in contravention of Ukraine's constitution. Article 73 of that document stipulates: "Alterations to the territory of Ukraine shall be resolved exclusively through the All-Ukraine referendum." Article 72 provides that only the Verkhovna Rada and the president can call a referendum and that a prerequisite is a petition signed by three million eligible voters, with at least 100,000 signatures collected from each of Ukraine's provinces and a majority backing the referendum in at least two-thirds of them.[3] The Crimea referendum, held while paramilitary forces and Russian troops roamed the streets, met none of these requirements. Moreover, the vote was organized by pro-Russian politicians who had recently seized power by force and whose leader's party, Russia Unity, won a mere four percent of the vote in the previous elections to the local parliament in October 2010.

Russian forces, both those already based in Crimea and others sent to reinforce them, started sealing off the peninsula and taking over installations. Amidst the upheaval, the referendum passed, and within days, Russia formally annexed Crimea with a "treaty of accession."

This initiated another chain reaction. Armed rebels in the eastern provinces of Donetsk and Luhansk (the Donbas region) seized installations, proclaimed republics, and readied for Crimea-like referendums, doubtless banking on Russia's backing. Ukraine seemed to be fragmenting. The Russian media began an information campaign to cast the Kyiv government in the worst light, linking it to the far-right and pro-Nazi forces of the 1940s and stoking the fears of the Russophone and ethnic Russian population in the Donbas. Speculation mounted about a Russian invasion in support of the insurgents.

Together, these unexpected events produced an atmosphere of emergency and the urgency of a genuine crisis.

Like most international political crises, this one was marked by mounting fears that war might soon erupt—and spread. Faced with a full-blown insurgency in Donetsk and Luhansk, the new Ukrainian government proclaimed an "anti-terrorism campaign" in April. Soon, Ukraine's army and National Guard, together with an array of private militias acting as free agents, were at war with the rebels, and the violence intensified after the May referendums on self-rule in the two eastern provinces. That, in turn, heightened the fear of a Russian invasion in support of the insurgents—especially as Moscow massed troops along Ukraine's border and staged military maneuvers in nearby Russian regions—even though Putin asked for the Donbas referendums to be delayed and failed to recognize the "republics" that were proclaimed in their aftermath. Estonia, Latvia, and Lithuania, the NATO members most directly exposed to a wider military confrontation, implored their allies for demonstrations of support, including the deployment of troops. The question became how Russia would react if NATO obliged.

Typically, opposing sides entangled in a crisis tend to believe—rightly or wrongly—that critical interests are at stake and that their adversaries will interpret signs of conciliation as weakness. This phenomenon was apparent in Ukraine, where the contending parties were disinclined to draw back and determined to demonstrate resolve. That mindset increased the tension, and with it the fear that misperception, faulty information, miscalculation, or even an accident would create a spiraling confrontation. There were (hyperbolic) comparisons between 2014 and August 1914.

What has come to pass in Ukraine—and what is still, as of this writing, underway—is a crisis for yet another reason: the rapid pace of developments and the sense of those caught up in them that, to paraphrase Ralph Waldo Emerson, "events are in the saddle," having acquired their own momentum and power. Those making critical decisions under such circumstances fear a loss of control. Entrenched assumptions harden, antagonists assume the worst, anxiety increases, and pessimism prevails. Ukraine has been no exception.

Thus Ukraine 2014 qualifies as classic crisis—indeed the worst to emerge between Russia and the West since the end of the Cold War—and one that will be explored and debated for decades to come. By the time it erupted, Western attitudes toward Russia had already begun to harden, thanks in large part to the 2008 Russia-Georgia war and Putin's tightening of political controls within Russia. President Obama's effort to improve the situation with a "reset" of relations with Russia was withering on the vine. This context made it even harder to calm the crisis, and the rhetorical salvos exchanged by Russia and the West did not help matters.

Amidst the rising political temperature, compromise by any of the contending parties risked being dismissed by critics as naïve, even pusillanimous. In all, it was an unpropitious setting for diplomacy.

But the crisis in Ukraine had even wider ramifications. Convinced that Russia's political support and supply of arms were the taproots of the Donbas insurgency, the United States and Europe imposed economic sanctions, which increased in severity in July after a Malaysia Airways passenger jet was shot down over eastern Ukraine (almost certainly by a missile fired by the insurgents at what they had assumed was a military aircraft), killing nearly 300 passengers and crew. Moscow responded to the sanctions with an amalgam of nonchalance and defiance, rolling out its own economic penalties and threatening more. The sanctions, the suspension of Russia from the G-8 bloc of global economic powers, and the cessation of NATO's political cooperation with Moscow shredded the relationship between Russia and the West and threatened the entire post–Cold War European political-military order. The larger imperative of cooperating to advance common interests fell by the wayside. Instead, in the press and among experts there was talk of a new Cold War, a colorful but facile comparison.

By late September 2014, when we wrote this introduction, the death toll in eastern Ukraine was making global headlines. Over three thousand people had been killed, and even more seemed destined to die.[4] The United Nations High Commission for Refugees estimated that many thousands more had fled their homes as refugees (mainly to Russia) or were "internally displaced persons." In Luhansk and Donetsk, people risked life and limb to continue quotidian routines. Food and other essential supplies were scarce, anxiety abundant. Russia continued to warn that it would not tolerate this state of affairs indefinitely and hinted at a "humanitarian intervention." On August 22, a convoy of Russian trucks with food and medicine crossed Ukraine's border without permission from the Ukrainian leadership, whose denunciation of the move as an invasion was echoed in the West. Worse still, five days later, Russian-supplied insurgent forces along with Russian troops opened a new front in Novoazovsk with the apparent aim of seizing the larger port city of Mariupol, which lies further west along the Sea of Azov's littoral, giving rise to predictions that Moscow was seeking a land corridor to Crimea. But more immediately, this gambit drew away some of the Ukrainian troops that had been advancing steadily against the rebels' positions in Donetsk and Luhansk and reducing the territory under their control. In the south, facing a rout, the Ukrainian army was soon in retreat; in the Donbas, it was forced to yield some of the ground it had gained.

By this time, the Donbas insurgents' leaders themselves were proclaiming publicly that several thousand Russians were fighting alongside them.[5] Reports broke that Russian armored units were transgressing the Ukrainian border and even engaging in combat, that artillery was being fired into Ukraine from Russian territory, and that Russia had ramped up the supply of arms to ensure that the rebels would remain a force to be reckoned with and could be used as leverage in political negotiations aimed at settling the crisis. Moscow seemed to believe that it could back the insurgents at arm's length and with plausible deniability. But the length of the arm was shrinking by the day, and the Kremlin's denials of direct and substantial military involvement were becoming steadily implausible. NATO was considering ways to improve the Ukrainian army's effectiveness and to establish bases and pre-position arms in the Baltic trio and Poland to ease mounting fears there.[6]

On September 5, Russia and Ukraine and the Donbas separatists signed a ceasefire agreement in Minsk, the capital of Belarus. Though the parliaments of the EU and Ukraine ratified the AA on September 16, its implementation was delayed to mid-December at the earliest, perhaps as a conciliatory gesture to Moscow. Yet fighting continued to rage, particularly in Donetsk, and the truce threatened to be ephemeral as reports persisted of indiscriminate shelling and of people being abducted, tortured, and killed by armed groups in the Donbas. There was no sign that the Donbas insurgents were open to a deal that would reincorporate the region into Ukraine; instead, they set about building their own political institutions and readying for elections while proclaiming that their ultimate aim was to join the Russian Federation. Nor was there any indication that Russia, despite the pressure of Western sanctions, was reconsidering its support for them.

This book represents a first cut at explaining the context, causes, and consequences of Ukraine 2014. It reflects all the challenges of writing about a conflagration that is still underway. Thus, while our book may be among the first book-length treatments of the topic, it will not be the last, let alone the definitive one. We are also well aware that some of our assessments will be overtaken by events and that some of our expectations will prove wrong. With time, everyone's understanding will improve as more studies appear. But the process must start somewhere. We have chosen to begin it with this book and at this moment.

We do not offer a blow-by-blow account of the crisis itself. What we provide in Chapter 2 is only an overview. Readers interested in fine-grained, day-by-day reportage must look to the work of the many fine journalists who have covered the crisis, with no small risk to their lives. Still, we do cover the salient points: the character of the Yanukovych government and its sources of internal and external support; the nature and extent of its pathologies (corruption and crony capitalism among them); the sources of popular discontent during Yanukovych's presidency; the nature and aims of the political opposition; and the moves made by Yanukovych, the opposition, Russia, and the West that were most critical to the initiation and expansion of the crisis.

Like every crisis, this one has a backstory and a context, and we explore them in Chapter 1 by surveying Ukraine's history and its relationship with Imperial, Soviet, and post-Soviet Russia. That complex history is centuries long. Numerous questions remain in dispute to this day, not least the nature of the relationship between the Ukrainian and Russian people and between their leaders. We are not historians and make no pretense of providing a full-scale history of Ukraine. Instead, we have tried to cover as many of the historical events, stages, and personalities that bear on the crisis as best we can so as to set the stage for the rest of the book. We are, as the footnotes show, indebted to many eminent historians of Ukraine.

The 2014 crisis in Ukraine was not foreordained—nothing in politics is—but the issues that divided the opposing parties are rooted in, and have been replayed during, Ukraine's lengthy history, albeit in varying forms. This is true of the controversy over Crimea. It is true as well of the divisions between Ukraine's west and center and its south and east. These differences involve an array of issues: the interpretation of critical events in Ukraine's history, policies pertaining to culture and language, Ukrainian-Russian relations, the question of who or what bears responsibility for the present crisis, and the outlook for Ukraine's future. A historical perspective also aids in understanding the political and economic challenges Ukraine has faced since its independence in 1991 and with which it will continue to struggle no matter the denouement of the 2014 crisis. For all of these reasons, Chapter 1 surveys Ukraine's Soviet past as well as its post-independence history, and often reaches further back in time. In short, Chapter 1 is an extended scene setter, while Chapter 2 discusses the current crisis itself.

Chapter 3 is devoted to Russia, which has been central to the crisis—and in the estimation of many observers, even caused it. In our view, that verdict is incomplete and exemplifies the single factor fallacy. This crisis involves too many participants for any one of them to be cast as the singular villain or hero. Moscow's decision to encourage—some would say suborn—the Crimean referendum, its annexation of Crimea, and its political and military support for the Donbas insurgency unquestionably ratcheted up the crisis and increased the hazard of a wider war. Yet it is important to understand why Russia did what it did, what the background and immediate context of its actions were, what it feared, what it wanted, and what price it was prepared to pay. Chapter 3 takes up these questions. It also uses the crisis as an opportunity to take stock of what kind of country Russia has become—politically, economically, socially, and militarily—since 1991 and how its evolution and present strengths and weaknesses influenced its interpretation of the crisis and the actions it took in response.

Chapter 4 looks to Europe. While we do discuss the assessments and actions of particular countries, in the main we use the EU and NATO (which is overwhelmingly European, even if American-led) as lenses for examining the considerations that shaped European perceptions and policies. We also contrast Europe's substantial commercial ties to Russia with the smaller magnitude of U.S.-Russian trade and investment and investigate the role that this difference in scale played in influencing Europe's attitude and actions. The chapter also examines the extent to which the crisis was shaped by EU and NATO policies toward East-Central Europe and Ukraine and other post-Soviet states. We look, in particular, at the EU's Eastern Partnership and NATO's eastward expansion and at how Russia perceived and responded to both of these initiatives. Again, in providing this background we are not claiming that EU and NATO policies in years past "caused" the crisis. Few things in international relations have a single cause; Ukraine 2014 is no exception.

Chapter 4 pays particular attention to NATO and its future. If there is one point of agreement among commentators on the Ukraine crisis, it is that it has presented NATO with its most serious post–Cold War test. That, of course, raises the question not only of how NATO will fare but also of what the crisis implies for an alliance that has been trying to define its purpose, formerly so clear, in a world without the Soviet Union. We are not convinced, as others have claimed, that the Ukraine crisis will make NATO more purposeful and cohesive.

In Chapter 5, we consider the outlook for Ukraine on the political, economic, and security fronts. We contend that it faces enormous challenges, all of which will be made even harder by the continuing Russia-backed insurgency in the Donbas and parts of the south. Two problems deserve—and get—particular attention: the war's effects on Ukraine's already beleaguered economy, and the prospects in war-torn areas for a political solution that combines economic reconstruction and political reconciliation. Because the crisis shows no sign of ending as we complete this book, it is impossible to be confident about a particular outcome. Hence we develop three scenarios for Ukraine and discuss their implications.

In Chapter 6, our conclusion, we argue that the 2014 crisis is about more than Ukraine. What has happened is a symptom of a much larger and more complicated problem, one that has received little attention from analysts and policymakers under-standably preoccupied with the immediate fallout from Rus-sia's annexation of Crimea and its multifaceted and growing support for the Donbas rebels. The larger lesson of the confla-gration in Ukraine is that there is no longer a European secu-rity architecture that Russia and the West recognize and are prepared to consider as providing rules of the road, however rough and ready. Certainly Russia has rejected it, and Moscow would doubtless respond that the West has not honored it either. The consensus underpinning a European security order may have been fraying before the crisis and was in any event embryonic and imperfect. But now it has been torn apart. In this respect, Ukraine 2014 is momentous in a way that Georgia 2008 was not.

The task facing Europe's leaders now is nothing less than fashioning a new European political and military order, one that makes crises like the one in Ukraine less likely, and easier to manage through prompt and effective diplomacy if they should erupt. Ukraine and Russia are fated by geography to live in close quarters. And economic realities—including, but not limited to, Ukraine's dependence on Russian energy—together with myr-iad historical and cultural legacies ensure that what one country does will continue to affect the other, for good or ill. The nature and magnitude of those effects will depend not merely on the modalities of the Russia-Ukraine relationship but also on the broader European order within which they unfold.

1 The Making of Ukraine

Visitors to Russia should not be surprised to learn from some of their interlocutors that Ukraine isn't really a nation, that it was part of Russia for centuries, and that its language is little more than Russian corrupted by Polish. Such sentiments are not limited to crackpots. At a 2008 NATO summit in Bucharest, Russian President Vladimir Putin said to President George W. Bush, "You don't understand, George, that Ukraine is not even a country."[1] In fact, Ukraine *is* a country and does have a history, and Ukrainians do have a distinctive identity. Yet central to the conflict between Ukraine and Russia—and to the politics of Ukraine itself—are disputes over interpretations of that history and the nature of that identity. Chief among these disputes are disagreements about what type of state Ukraine should have and what its relationship toward Russia and the West should be.

Much of Ukraine's history unfolded outside Russia: non-Russian empires and states ruled large chunks of Ukrainian-populated territories for centuries. As a result, Ukraine always was, and still remains, regionally, culturally, and politically diverse. No European—and certainly no non-European—state has ever been homogeneous. Ukraine's heterogeneity is the historical norm, not the historical exception.

Nevertheless, for reasons of history, culture, and above all geography, the choices Ukraine makes in domestic and foreign policy will always affect its northeastern neighbor. Propinquity to Russia ensures that the Russian factor will be a perennial consideration in Ukraine's politics and economics.

The East-West Divide

One of the most contentious issues in Ukraine is the extent and nature of its integration with the West. Broadly speaking, alignment with the West resonates most strongly in central and western Ukraine, while support for Russia predominates in the south and east. Ukrainians in the east and south are more closely connected—culturally, emotionally, and politically—to Russia than their fellow citizens are. This is true especially of Ukraine's ethnic Russians, who accounted for 18 percent of the population before the 2014 war in the Donbas. Over 80 percent lived in the south and east and, according to the 2001 census, accounted for nearly 30 percent of the population in the eastern provinces of Donetsk, Luhansk, Kharkiv, Dnipropetrovs'k, and Zaporizhzhia (down from 36 percent in 1989).[2]

These numbers should not be taken as evidence that all Russians in Ukraine, let alone all eastern Ukrainians, wish to secede. Separatism has had strong appeal in Crimea thanks to its history, the significant presence of World War II veterans and their families within its Russian population, and the fact that it is Ukraine's sole Russian-majority province. In the Donbas, by contrast, even while proposals for autonomy via federalization have attracted significant support, calls for abandoning Ukraine and uniting with Russia, or for proclaiming independence, have not. What occurred in Crimea—a referendum followed by

Russian annexation—is therefore unlikely to occur in the east. Ukraine's famed "east-west divide" should therefore be placed in perspective.[3]

There are large linguistic and political differences between Ukraine's westernmost and easternmost provinces, but the intervening space is marked by subtle gradations, making it inaccurate to say that the two halves of the country, separated by the Dnipro River (Russian: Dnepr), are homogeneous and irreconcilably antagonistic. Nor is regionalism the only division that matters in Ukraine. As they do elsewhere, distinctions based on class, gender, urbanism, and secularism matter too. Easterners and westerners are not monolithic in their political views, and ethnicity is not a straightforward predictor of sentiments toward Russia. In short, the broad characterization of eastern Ukraine as pro-Russian is simplistic.

Still, it would be wrong to dismiss the differences between the west and center and the south and east, which are artifacts of Ukraine's complex history. They have surfaced, as we shall see, numerous times since 1991, notably during election campaigns, the 2004 Orange Revolution, and the periodic agitations by eastern political forces demanding official status for the Russian language, autonomy, and even secession. These differences also reveal themselves in interpretations of pivotal events and personalities in Ukraine's long history.

Post-Soviet Russian nationalists started contesting Crimea's status as early as 1992. On May 21, Russia's parliament declared illegal the 1954 transfer of the peninsula to Soviet Ukraine from the Russian Soviet Federated Socialist Republic (RSFSR). Earlier in May 1992, with Russia's encouragement, Crimea's legislature passed an independence resolution by 118 to 28 and scheduled an August referendum to bring it before voters.[4] Two years later, the chamber,

again with Moscow's approval, adopted a constitution stipu-
lating independence. That crisis was resolved in 1996, when
Crimea became an autonomous republic with considerable powers of self-rule within Ukraine.

Crimea was not the sole example of the divide between east and
west: there was also the fall 1992 campaign in Donetsk to declare
Russian the second official language and the June 1993 Donbas
miners' strike, which, while fundamentally an economic protest,
included demands for local autonomy.[5] As the 1994 elections for
the Verkhovna Rada (Ukraine's parliament, Rada for short) neared,
the Donetsk and Luhansk provincial assemblies held referendums,
which won wide support, on federalization, elevating the status of
Russian, and deepening Ukraine's integration with the Russia-led
Commonwealth of Independent States. The elections themselves
offered additional proof of the divergent political orientation of
the west and the center, where pro-Ukrainian parties did well, and
the south and the east, which remained strongholds of the pro-
Russian communists and other leftist parties.

The Assemblage of Ukraine

Ukrainians generally trace their nationhood and statehood to
the Kyivan Rus' state that existed from the ninth to the thirteenth centuries in the area roughly comprising today's Ukraine,
Belarus, and western Russia. So do Belarusians and Russians. The
latter, in particular, consider Kyiv (Russian: Kiev) the "Mother
of Russian cities." Ukrainians are apt to counter with the claim
that Kyiv is the capital of today's Ukraine and is situated in the
heart of ethnically Ukrainian territory, similar to Rome's place in
Italians' conceptions of their history. They are also apt to insist
that the decline of Kyivan Rus' and its eventual destruction by

the Mongols constituted a loss of statehood, not of national identity. They would also note the revival of Ukrainian statehood in the seventeenth and eighteenth centuries, in the form of the various Cossack (Ukrainian: Kozak) polities associated, most notably, with such Hetmans, or leaders, as Bohdan Khmelnytsky and Ivan Mazepa. The absorption of the Hetman states by Imperial Russia and the Polish-Lithuanian Commonwealth represents, in this narrative, the second time that statehood was lost while nationhood endured.

By the seventeenth and eighteenth centuries, the lands of contemporary Ukraine and the forebears of today's Ukrainians were parceled out among Poland, Russia, the Ottoman Empire, and the Habsburg Empire, a consequence of wars and the rise and fall of empires and states. As the noted historian of Ukraine Roman Szporluk tells us, prior to the 1660s, the bulk of the spaces inhabited by Ukrainians was under Polish rule, within the Polish-Lithuanian Commonwealth, and extended beyond the Dnipro River, encompassing Kyiv.[6] Even after the gains Russia made at Poland's expense—and that were recorded in the 1667 Treaty of Andrusovo, which ended a war of over thirteen years between Russia and the Polish-Lithuanian Commonwealth—only the areas corresponding to two of present-day Ukraine's provinces, Chernihiv and Poltava, along with the city of Kyiv, passed to the Russian Tsar. (See Figure 1.1.) Ukrainians west of the Dnipro remained under Polish rule; most were peasants who worked the vast latifundia owned by Polish noblemen-landlords and administered by Jews. The partitions of the Polish-Lithuanian Commonwealth between 1772 and 1795 transferred more of its Ukrainian-populated lands to Russia, but the Austrian Habsburgs annexed some as well. In the Austrian province of Galicia, Poles predominated in the west, Ukrainians (known as Ruthenians or

Figure 1.1
Ukrainian provinces.

Rusyns) in the east, though the Poles still lorded it over Ukraini-ans in eastern Galicia. The Habsburg province of Volhynia too contained Ukrainians, albeit a minority.

Ukrainians would be redistributed yet again after World War I, this time among the states that rose from the ruins of the Habsburg, Russian, and Ottoman empires. Eastern Galicia became part of a new Polish state that was reconstituted under the post-war settlement. Czechoslovakia gained Transcarpathia (today's Zakarpattia province in the west), which it then lost to Nazi-allied Hungary in 1939. Romania absorbed what now corresponds to Ukraine's Chernivtsi province. These territories would not be incorporated into the Soviet Union until Stalin invaded Poland following his 1939 "non-aggression" pact with

Adolf Hitler. (Ukrainians generally welcomed the Soviet advance into eastern Poland, believing that it would free them from Polish rule and lead to independence rather than ending in incorporation into the USSR.[7]) In fact, war with Germany, following Hitler's decision to go to war against the USSR in 1941, interrupted the absorption of these lands, which was completed only following the USSR's final victory on the eastern front in 1945.

The interim years were marked by bewildering and bloody complexity.[8] Ukrainian nationalist organizations—the branches of the Organization of Ukrainian Nationalists (OUN) led by Stepan Bandera and Andrii Melnyk—turned on one another with ferocity. The defeated Melnyk wing collaborated with the Nazis in the (misplaced) hope that doing so would enable the creation of a Ukrainian state once the war ended. The Bandera group briefly cooperated with the Germans but then fought them, as well as Soviet partisans and the Red Army, for the same objective: statehood. Many Ukrainians joined Nazi police forces and helped in the destruction of Galician and Volhynian Jews. The OUN-Bandera's fighting arm, the Ukrainian Insurgent Army (UPA), expelled (and killed) en masse Poles from Galicia and Volhynia because it considered these territories parts of a future Ukrainian homeland and viewed Poles as conquerors and interlopers.[9] That violence provoked harsh reprisals from Polish partisans and ignited a pitiless civil war between the two nationalities. This bloody conflict compounded the deportations and mass murders perpetrated during the successive occupations by the Soviet Union, Nazi Germany, and again by the Soviet Union, between 1939 and 1945.

Ukraine's south and parts of its east—including Crimea (home since the fifteenth century to the Crimean Tatars), Odessa, Mykolaiv, Kherson, Donetsk, and Dnipropetrovs'k—had a different history. They were joined to Russia after being wrested from the Ottoman Empire in 1783 by Catherine the Great, and came to be known as "Novorossiya" (New Russia). This moniker has now reappeared in the lexicon of Russian nationalists favoring eastern Ukraine's secession (à la Crimea) or a federal arrangement that offers autonomy from Kyiv. The term is also used by the insurgents who have proclaimed "republics" in Luhansk and Donetsk. Putin himself used the term twice in 2014: during his annual marathon public Q&A in April and again in the title of his August address to Russian-backed separatist fighters in Ukraine.[10] The Russian president has asserted—and he is not alone—that Ukraine's claim to these territories is tenuous because they were allocated to the Ukrainian Soviet Socialist Republic only in the 1920s (along with Crimea three decades later). Now that Russia has absorbed Crimea, if "Novorossiya" were to become a Russian-sponsored statelet comparable to the former Georgian territories of Abkhazia and South Ossetia, or if it were to be annexed by Russia, Ukraine would lose its coastline, some 20 million in population, and its most industrialized regions.[11] So what may appear an abstract debate about history's fine points in fact carries serious implications.

This historical sketch shows that Ukrainian lands, on the whole, have not always been ruled by Russia. Some lands, mainly those gained from Poland in 1667, have indeed been ruled by Russia for 300 years, but the rest remained outside Imperial Russia and the Soviet Union for long stretches, in some instances until the end of World War II. Modern Ukrainian nationalism started to emerge in the nineteenth century, kindled by an intellectual and cultural symbiosis between Ukrainians living under Polish and Russian rule and Ukrainian intellectuals from the Russian Empire. Among these figures were Mikhaylo Drahomanov and Mikhaylo Hrushevsky, who contributed in ways similar to their western counterparts, such as the poet and writer Ivan Franko, for whom the city and province of Ivano-Frankivsk are named. As in most Eastern European countries, intellectuals and clergy led the way, mobilizing a predominantly peasant population and working to construct a national identity distinct from those of the two overlords, Poland and Russia.

These nationalizing projects were conditioned by the political, economic, and cultural circumstances prevailing in the empires that ruled their respective parts of Ukraine. Ukrainians in the west were well governed by the Habsburgs and, from the 1920s, less well by Poland, and lived very different lives from those of their Russian-ruled eastern kin.[12] Under the Habsburgs, and to a lesser extent under Poland, Ukrainians had their schools, publications, civic organizations, and political parties, and the Ukrainian Greek Catholic Church was recognized. In a word, the political world was liberal by the standards of the time. Not surprisingly, when the Red Army drove Nazi troops from Ukrainian territories, the fiercest armed resistance to Stalin's annexation of the Ukrainian-majority areas of eastern Poland arose in the west. (The resistance failed but lingered into the early 1950s.) In the east, by contrast, many Ukrainian intellectuals, gentry, clergy, and professionals were Russified, whether by choice or as a consequence of Imperial Russian policies, by the nineteenth century; tsarist decrees banned the Ukrainian language until the early twentieth century, and the Ukrainian Orthodox Church was subsumed by its Russian counterpart.

Ukrainian states emerged amidst the upheavals created by World War I. Following the fall of the Habsburg Empire, the Western Ukrainian People's Republic was proclaimed in Eastern Galicia, but it soon lost the province to Polish troops. Three successive Ukrainian polities sprouted in the east—owing to events too complex to cover here—but failed because of their inability to establish effective state and military institutions, because of the inchoate nationalism of Russian-ruled Ukrainians, and, in one instance, because of the defeat of Germany, which had acted as the polity's sponsor. Although the Ukrainian national movement that emerged in Kyiv enjoyed significant support among the intelligentsia (and to a lesser degree the peasants), it was no match for the armies of the Russian Bolsheviks and their enemies, the Whites. Moreover, the Bolsheviks had considerable support in the Russified and industrialized east, especially among the working class. The leaders of western and eastern Ukraine even cooperated briefly to form a single state, but it proved tenuous, not least because Ukraine's lands became a venue for savage wars involving Polish, Bolshevik, and White Russian forces as well as anarchists, bandits, marauders, and warlords. Increasingly, the Ukrainian national movement became marginalized on its own territory. When Poland and Soviet Russia fought over the territories that lay between them after World War I and struck a deal in 1921, the Poles abandoned the Ukrainian forces of Symon Petliura with which they had aligned in hopes of gaining an independent state. Ukrainians' quest for statehood again came to naught. Under the Treaty of Riga, some four million of them were apportioned to Poland.[13] The rest became part of the Ukrainian Soviet Socialist Republic, with its capital in Kharkiv and later Kyiv, which by the latter half of the 1920s contained 26 million people.

Ukrainian language and culture were revived during the short-lived period of *korenizatsiya* ("nativization") in the 1920s, but with Stalin's consolidation of unrivalled power, both were transformed into a medium for instilling "socialist conscious-ness" and conformity to an ideology that was Ukrainian in form, socialist in content, and intolerant of nationalism. The famine of 1932–1933 (now known to many Ukrainians as the Holodomor), which coincided with a rollback of nativization and the brutal repression of the Ukrainian intelligentsia and Ukrainians in the communist part suspected of nationalism, marked Soviet Ukraine's transformation into an appendage of Moscow.

The next big expansion of Soviet Ukraine's boundaries occurred in late 1939, when, as a result of the Soviet-Nazi partition of Poland, eastern Poland was "liberated" and its Belarusian- and Ukrainian-populated territories adjoined to the Belorussian and Ukrainian SSRs (Soviet Socialist Repub-lics). Soviet historiography celebrated western Ukraine's incorporation into the USSR as a "progressive" achievement, one that would be finalized starting in mid-1943, once the Red Army turned the tide against Nazi Germany following the epic battle of Stalingrad. A final territorial reallocation took place in 1954, when, on Nikita Khrushchev's initiative, the USSR Supreme Soviet transferred Crimea—then within the RSFSR—to the Ukrainian SSR, a decision that post-Soviet Russian nationalists would denounce as a wrong that required righting.

As we shall see, the divergent experiences of western Ukrai-nians and their kin in the south and east have left their mark on independent Ukraine in the form of differences on mat-ters ranging from identity and internal politics to foreign policy. These differences would reemerge in 2013–2014 and segue into a clash between Russia and the West over Ukraine's future.

Revolution from Above

Ukrainian independence became a reality in 1991 following the unexpected implosion of the Soviet Union. But it would be uncharitable as well as inaccurate to say that Ukraine's independence (and that of the other thirteen non-Russian post-Soviet states) was delivered from above rather than won from below; if it was helped by the dissolution of the USSR, it was helped as well by intrepid individuals, mass demonstrations, numerous and variegated civic organizations, patriotically inclined local communists, and intellectuals animated by wide-ranging discussions of once-banned topics. This ground-level ferment was particularly powerful in the Baltic states (Estonia, Latvia, and Lithuania), the South Caucasus (Armenia, Azerbaijan, and Georgia), and Ukraine. But it would never have been tolerated in the unreformed Soviet Union, where dissent was a ticket to imprisonment, exile, or worse. The difference was that the political changes in Moscow that unleashed these destabilizing forces also stayed the hand of state repression.

Those changes, which surprised even seasoned observers of the Soviet Union, began in 1985, when the new head of the Soviet communist party, Mikhail Gorbachev, and other like-minded leaders decided to reform the system in order to save it. The purpose of *perestroika* and *glasnost'*, Gorbachev's catchwords for economic restructuring and political liberalization, was to create a new, rejuvenated socialist order featuring economic dynamism and increased political openness and to end "the period of stagnation," as the last years of Leonid Brezhnev's long rule came to be known. The attempt to reform a sclerotic system from above enabled challenges from below to gain strength and to shake—and eventually dismantle—the Soviet colossus.

Even the most reform-minded leaders inside Gorbachev's circle did not, of course, intend this denouement. The "Gorbachev phenomenon," as Moshe Levin called it, exemplified the law of unintended consequences and vindicated the wisdom of Alexis de Tocqueville's observation that revolutions arise not when stagnation persists but when change commences.[14]

Gorbachev's program created consternation among conservatives and incited feuds between the friends and foes of change, the more so once the system was under siege. The dramatic debates in the media revealing the Soviet leaders' numerous failings, blunders, and cruelties were rapidly denuding the system's legitimacy and its capacity to control events. In the summer of 1989, Eastern Europe's communist regimes fell in rapid succession, and, in contrast to Hungary in 1956 and Czechoslovakia in 1968, Soviet tanks were not dispatched to crush the revolts. Those signal events emboldened opposition forces within the Soviet Union. Boris Yeltsin, having already broken with Gorbachev, resigned from the communist party in 1990 and started setting the political pace in the Russian Republic, the heart of the Soviet Union, in cooperation with radical reformers in the other republics.

The tremors Gorbachev's reforms created in the Soviet Union's center soon pervaded the periphery. In 1988 mass demonstrations began in the Baltic republics, and independence was on the agenda. Once the protest rallies spread to Ukraine— the most consequential republic next to the RSFSR—the Soviet Union's days were numbered. The protests started in the bastion of Ukrainian nationalism and anti-communism, Lviv, drawing tens of thousands of people onto the streets. Soon, the demonstrations swept eastward and reached Kyiv, the capital, and other parts of central Ukraine. The south and the east (the Donbas), where the communist party's conservative elements exercised more control, were quiet by comparison. Still, by 1989 most of Ukraine was awash in political agitation.

Ukraine was the most important of the fourteen non-Russian Soviet republics for several reasons. Together with the RSFSR and Belorussia, it constituted the Slavic trio, which evoked memories of the Eastern Slav's first state, Kyivan Rus'. Ukraine was also the second most populous Soviet republic. It guarded the Soviet Union's western frontier and served as a corridor to Soviet-controlled Eastern Europe. Comparable to France in size and to Italy in population, it contained some 50 million people. It was rich in raw materials, its east brimmed with industries and mines, and, thanks to its famed "black earth," it was also a breadbasket. It was an important producer of armaments as well. On the cultural-historical front, Ukraine was central to the emergence of Russian civilization and the formation of Kyivan Rus'. Not for nothing did Gorbachev remark that without Ukraine there could be no Soviet Union.[15]

Ukraine: High Politics

The Ukrainian communist party's boss, Volodymyr Shcherbytsky, deemed Gorbachev's reforms misguided, even dangerous. In 1989, Shcherbytsky, aged, ill, and demoralized, resigned; he died the following year. Following brief stints by two lackluster successors, the spotlight shifted to the man who would play a decisive part in Ukraine's independence, the second secretary of the Ukrainian communist party and its counter-propaganda chief, Leonid Kravchuk. Unlike Shcherbytsky and his two immediate successors, whose roots were in the Russified Donbas, Kravchuk had been born in the west (in Volhynia), had first-hand experience of the Ukrainian nationalist resistance, and spoke fluent Ukrainian. As the party's counter-propagandist, he was also conversant with the language and logic of "bourgeois nationalism," which he soon adopted.

Kravchuk's background worried party conservatives, particularly those from the Donbas. They thought his conciliatory approach toward the political opposition was a formula for disaster because it seemed to legitimate and encourage increasingly influential anti-Soviet forces. Their fears were not unwarranted. In the March 1990 elections to Ukraine's parliament (Verkhovna Rada)—after which Kravchuk was chosen as chairman of the legislature—the non-communist opposition had fared well and become a force to be reckoned with. The opposition's success in finding common ground with reform-minded communists and ex-communists strengthened them further. Most Ukrainian opposition leaders still had not publicly called for independence and instead sought greater autonomy within a Soviet Union reconceived as a true federation. Yet independence was becoming a real possibility, and to many, an inevitability. That made the communist conservatives doubly suspicious of Kravchuk: they feared that his conciliatory tactics would eventually destroy the communist party's seventy-year political monopoly and thus the Soviet Union itself.

Ukraine: Low Politics

The Gorbachev phenomenon, the battle between reformers and conservatives in Moscow and in several Soviet republics, elections that weakened the communist party's grip, and the comings and goings of leaders—these were all part of the drama that would culminate in an independent Ukraine. But Ukraine's sovereignty also resulted from socioeconomic changes on the ground that both shaped and were enabled by elite-level politics.

Foremost among these was the deepening economic crisis, which strengthened the anti-Soviet forces and weakened the system's defenders. While it had many causes, the overarching one was that Gorbachev's reforms had disrupted the established economic order based on centralized planning and allocation but failed to create a working alternative. In part, this was because Gorbachev and his fellow reformers lacked a clear conception, beyond generalities, of what they wanted to do, and how. Yes, they wanted to reenergize the socialist project by making it more efficient, productive, and free. To this end they favored decentralizing decision-making and permitting more leeway for private property and market forces. But beyond that, their aims were fuzzy. What was clear was that they had no intention of creating a capitalist system in which the state's role was pared down to running a few sectors of the economy, providing basic social services, and playing a regulatory role while private property and supply and demand did the rest, all within a multi-party polity.

The reforms had many unforeseen and counterproductive consequences. The liberalization of prices, however limited, made many essential goods costlier for consumers. The subsidies that continued to flow to state companies so that they could avoid politically perilous layoffs strengthened inflation. Inflation, in turn, created an underground economy in which scarce goods could be obtained at high prices and through good connections. A mismatch arose between people's cash savings and bank deposits and retirees' pensions, on the one hand, and the inflation rate, on the other. The latter was below 5 percent when Gorbachev took the helm; by 1991 it had reached 200 percent.[16]

Foreign debt, which totaled $800 million in 1988, soared to a net $46 billion in 1990.[17]

These disruptions soon reached Ukraine.[18] By 1992, its economy had shrunk by a fifth and inflation had reached 2,500 percent. Scarcity and skyrocketing prices increased the already enormous corruption. The percentage of Ukrainians living in poverty rose from 15 percent in 1989 to 50 percent by 1992. The disruption of supply networks made seeds and machinery scarce and unaffordable to farmers. Ukraine's coal, steel, and heavy industries slumped given their dependence on demand from other parts of the Soviet Union, particularly the Russian heartland, which also struggled to maintain production and employment. The Donbas was hit especially hard. A reform-induced economic revival might have shored up support for the Soviet system. But it proved elusive, and the communist party became a symbol of rudderlessness. An increasing number of Ukrainians began to wonder whether independence, which would provide local control over economic decisions, was the way out of the mess.

On the political front, *glasnost'* permitted the emergence of numerous Ukrainian civic and cultural organizations. As demoralization gained grounds in the communist party ranks—in 1989, 6,200 cadres resigned from the Ukrainian party and in 1990, 251,000—non-party organizations filled the political vacuum.[19] Thousands were formed with breathtaking speed, with reformists and nationalists in the forefront. Leading the charge was the Ukrainian Popular Movement, or Rukh, whose founding congress in September 1989 attracted nearly 3,000 participants. Nationalist organizations such as Rukh were overwhelmingly ethnic Ukrainian in membership and rooted in the west. They had little purchase in the Russified south and east. Unsurprisingly, coal miners emerged as a political force in the Donbas.

Among the consequences of the birth of civil society was the exploration of historical topics that were proscribed or on which there was a mandatory official line.[20] The 1932–1933 Ukrainian famine—the Holodomor—was one of them.[21] In a sign of the times, official documents pertaining to it were released for the first time, leading many to conclude that the Stalinist system had employed the famine—which, according to current demographic estimates, killed three to four million Ukrainian peasants—to destroy Ukrainian nationalism.[22] Reinterpretations of the late 1920s and the 1930s focused on the resistance to collectivization, on the killing and mass arrests and deportations of the peasantry, and on the show trials and executions that decimated the Ukrainian intelligentsia and the local communist party during the Stalinist purges. The Western Ukrainian People's Republic, in formerly Habsburg lands, and the Ukrainian People's Republic, in formerly tsarist lands—both treated in Soviet historiography as retrograde and "bourgeois-nationalist"—were reassessed as participants in a heroic, though ill-fated, phase in the Ukrainian nation's long quest for self-determination. The traditional symbols of the Ukrainian national movement, the yellow and blue banner and the trident, reappeared, as did its anthem, "Ukraine Still Lives." Figures associated with Ukrainian nationalism, such as Mikhaylo Hrushevsky, Ivan Franko, Symon Petliura, and the left-leaning writer Volodymyr Vynnychenko (a leader in one of the ephemeral post-World War I Ukrainian states) became iconic. The revisionism reached even further into the past, focusing on Hetman Bohdan Khmelnytsky's ill-fated alliance with Muscovy in 1654 and the defeat of Hetman Ivan Mazepa (and his Swedish allies) at Russian hands at Poltava in 1709. This reconsideration of the past and reimagining of the future had the most resonance in western and central Ukraine.

None of these fresh-eyed forays into history occurred without controversy. Particularly sensitive were positive reassessments of the nationalist movement in wartime and post-war western Ukraine—especially of the OUN and the UPA, and nationalist leaders such as Stepan Bandera. Both organizations had been portrayed in Soviet historical accounts as the tools of quislings, fascists, and killers of Russians, Poles, and Jews in Volhynia and Galicia. Recasting these figures in a positive light looked to some like an attempt to prettify World War II nationalists; it stirred hostility, especially in the Russophone south and east, where separatism had already gained appeal. In Crimea, it had already become a topic of discussion, and a January 1991 referendum on "restoring the Crimean ASSR [Autonomous Soviet Socialist Republic] as a subject of the USSR" was approved by 93 percent of voters.[23] This vote, together with the campaign to nullify Crimea's 1954 transfer to Ukraine, put Kyiv on notice that Ukrainian independence could spawn secessionist movements.

Nationalist sentiment was further stoked by public anger over industrialization's desecration of the natural environment. The damage was easily portrayed as the result of an economic model that had been forced on Ukraine. The explosion at Chornobyl, less than a hundred miles north of Kyiv, on April 26, 1986, crystallized these concerns about the toxic impact of politics on the environment and lent further credence to claims that Ukraine, far from having been a beneficiary of Soviet modernization, was a prime victim.

Religion, too, fueled Ukrainian nationalism. Churches that had been banned—the Ukrainian Greek Catholic Church and the Ukrainian Autocephalous Orthodox Church (UAOC)—reemerged. The Soviet regime had treated them as purveyors of secessionist and anti-Soviet sentiment that were, moreover, connected to anti-communist organizations in the Ukrainian diaspora. Their revival, their campaigns to reclaim lost parishes and properties, and their success in attracting worshippers, along with the return of exiled church leaders, strengthened nationalist sentiments, above all in western Ukraine. The reappearance of the UAOC, in particular, threatened the dominance the Moscow-based Russian Orthodox Patriarchate had long enjoyed in Ukraine through its local affiliate, the Ukrainian Orthodox Church (UOC). (The Moscow Patriarchate's problems would increase following Ukraine's independence and the appearance of the Ukrainian Orthodox Church–Kyiv Patriarchate, which rejected the Moscow patriarch's authority and was welcomed by independent Ukraine's first president, Leonid Kravchuk.)

The Endgame

As 1990 ended, the USSR's dissolution was a matter of when, not if. In October, strikes and protests erupted across Ukraine. Among the demands were calls for Ukrainian soldiers to be stationed only within Ukraine, new elections to the Rada, and the confiscation of the communist party's properties. In March 1991, Gorbachev made a last-ditch effort to save the union by calling a referendum, but it yielded a mixed result. In Ukraine, 70 percent of voters approved his proposal for a revamped federation, but 80 percent supported Ukraine's autonomy, which meant that Ukrainian laws would supersede Moscow's. And in July, following the pattern in other republics, the Rada established a Ukrainian presidency.

Important as these developments were, the decisive blow came on August 19, 1991, in Moscow. While Gorbachev was vacationing in the Crimea, his opponents placed him under house arrest and formed an Emergency Committee, clearly a prelude to a clampdown aimed at rolling back the revolution. But Yeltsin rallied the opposition in Moscow, demonstrations erupted in various republics, and within three days the coup had collapsed. By the end of the year so had the USSR.

Kravchuk had hedged his bets and avoided condemning the coup leaders until well after their failure was evident.[24] But, ever the nimble political operator, he gave fulsome support to the Rada's declaration of independence on August 24. By contrast, President George H.W. Bush and his administration clung to hopes that the USSR might survive as a loose federation. It was too late for that. On December 1, a referendum on Ukraine's independence was approved by 90 percent of the voters. Though it won a majority in all of Ukraine's provinces, the margin was noticeably smaller in Crimea (54 percent) and the eastern provinces. Simultaneously, Kravchuk was elected president, besting four other candidates and garnering nearly 62 percent of the vote.

A week later, the presidents of the Slavic troika—Belorussia's Stanislau Sushkevich, Russia's Yeltsin, and Ukraine's Kravchuk—gathered at a hunting lodge in the Belovezh forest in western Belorussia. Gorbachev had proposed a new Union, and Yeltsin and Sushkevich had come prepared, in principle, to discuss a possible arrangement along these lines. But Kravchuk would have none of it and reminded them that Ukraine had chosen independence in the recent referendum. As he recalled later, "I arrived armed with the expression of all-Ukrainian will. Moreover, I already possessed the status of president."[25] He acted like one and forbade the Ukrainian delegation from participating in the drafting of documents that backtracked on independence. In the end, the Slavic trio declared the Commonwealth

of Independent States, a formulation whose practical effect was
the death of the Soviet Union—and the definitive independence
of Ukraine.

Independent Ukraine

Overnight, Ukraine had become a "post-communist" country.
But what precisely did that mean?[26] On this there was little consensus. Some parties favored the consolidation of democracy
and the initiation of market-oriented economic reform, but
none of them had become a national force. Though banned, the
communist party was not dead; it reconstituted itself in 1993
and won more votes—3 million, three times as many as its nearest rival won—than any other party in the 1994 Rada elections.
And the communists had no enthusiasm for democracy or capitalism. They and their parliamentary partners, the Socialist Party
and the Peasant Party, feared that a march to the market would
produce more poverty and inequality, adding to the already
severe economic insecurity. The continuing economic collapse
of the 1990s spread that insecurity and ensured leftist parties
a solid electoral base, especially in the industrialized, Russified
south and east. (See Figure 1.2.)

This lack of consensus in newly independent Ukraine reflected,
in part, Ukraine's seven decades of Soviet rule, and before that
Ukrainians' history of having lived apart in empires and states
that differed culturally and politically. The Soviet legacy also
affected Ukrainians' notion of who they were. Ukraine was now
a national state. But the meaning of "national" was ambiguous.
Did it connote a state for the Ukrainian nation or for the people of Ukraine? For many, especially in the western and central
provinces, Ukraine's adoption of the national movement's flag,

trident, and anthem represented the realization of a dream: a Ukrainian nation-state. [27] Most nationalists were willing to grant language and cultural rights to Ukraine's non-Ukrainian ethnic groups, but minority nationalities such as Jews, Crimean Tatars, and Russians were skittish about "Ukrainianization." Jews had adopted an urbanized culture and identity that had historically been Russian. Crimean Tatars were happy to be in Ukraine rather than Russia (Stalin had expelled them from Crimea during the war), but they wanted to revive their own language and culture within their historic homeland. The sentiments of Ukraine's ethnic Russians were—and remain—particularly important, as they accounted for 36 percent of the population on average of the five eastern provinces of Donetsk, Luhansk, Kharkiv, Dnipropetrovs'k, and Zaporizhzhia.[28] Then there were the

Figure 1.2
Ethnic majorities throughout Ukraine.

ethnic Ukrainians who regarded Russian as their first language and were concentrated overwhelmingly in the south and east.

Ukrainian elites attempted to unify these disparate constituencies by declaring Ukraine a state of all of its citizens, whatever their nationality, while committing themselves to the promotion of Ukrainian as a state language. This formulation seemed a reasonable compromise, but it did little to assuage those who wanted Russian to be recognized as the second official language. But that solution would have been thin gruel for Ukrainian nationalists, who yearned for a state and society bearing the stamp of the Ukrainian language and culture and who feared that the state's commitment to promoting both would amount to lip service.

Ukrainians considered themselves Europeans, but that too was hazy. For some, Europeanism required that Ukraine cooperate with the European Union and NATO in hopes of eventually joining both; they regarded alignment with Russia as tantamount to a turn away from Europe and a reversion to Russian hegemony. Europe itself had no coherent plan for Ukraine in the early 1990s, let alone one involving EU and NATO membership. Moreover, European leaders noted Moscow's aversion to the eastward extension of western economic and military organizations. For other Ukrainians, principally in the east and south, Europeanism connoted greater cooperation with Russia, with which they felt a strong kinship based on history, language, and culture. But integration with Russia could not easily be reconciled with EU and NATO membership and, in any event, would have been unpopular in western and central Ukraine. In short, Ukrainians' conceptions of foreign policy were inseparable from their various conceptions of national identity and statehood.

The Kravchuk Years

Kravchuk managed his country's east-west divisions deftly, preventing them from precipitating a bloody breakup. And he found a stopgap solution to a closely related problem: the Russian Black Sea Fleet's future rights to its base, the Crimean port of Sevastopol. In 1992, he and Russian president Yeltsin signed an agreement on joint control of the flotilla that deferred a decision on basing rights for three years, but Kravchuk rejected Russian ownership of any part of Crimea.[29] The January 1994 Trilateral Statement, signed by Russia, the United States, and Ukraine addressed concerns about a nuclear-armed Ukraine. The accord enabled Ukraine to transfer its Soviet-era nuclear weapons to Russia—completed in 1996—and to accede to the Nuclear Non-Proliferation Treaty.[30] The deal was sweetened by American economic aid and security guarantees. The latter were strengthened in December when the three leaders, together with the British prime minister, signed the Budapest Memorandum that included a pledge "to respect the independence and existing borders of Ukraine."[31] Under Kravchuk, Ukraine also established a national army out of the Soviet military units on its territory, and its diplomatic missions abroad grew apace. Together, these measures consolidated the external elements of Ukraine's independence.

Kravchuk's economic record, by contrast, was dismal. As the economist Anders Åslund has written, "Economic policy could not have been more disastrous. No postcommunist country was hit by such hyperinflation and such a huge decline without war as Ukraine. . . . No market economy was built, and a sheer minimum of privatization was undertaken. An entrenched machine of rent-seeking was established."[32] The statistics bear out this verdict. Ukraine's inflation rate leaped to 10,000 percent by

1993, and its economy contracted by 60 percent in the 1990s. Nominal wages surged, accelerating price increases and bloating the budget deficit, but real wages plummeted by 63 percent between 1990 and 1993.[33] Nearly a third of Ukrainians lived in poverty, particularly villagers, the aged, and retirees.[34] A struggling, shrinking middle class survived by working multiple jobs, buying goods abroad and reselling them at home, or laboring as caregivers in Europe and construction workers in Russia. Amidst this penury a super-rich elite surfaced, gaming the system and creating the corruption and cronyism, the politics and economics of oligarchy that still endure in Ukraine.

Kravchuk's government was hobbled by two additional factors. First, he had to focus on strengthening Ukraine as a state and on consolidating its security, issues that became urgent following the USSR's collapse. Second, neither his government nor Ukraine's elite then consisted of market-oriented reformers: the nationalist opposition focused on issues of culture, identity, and state-creation, while the communists were hostile to the market. As a result, while Eastern Europe's post-communist countries moved toward the market, Ukraine remained mired in a no-man's land between a centrally planned economy that no longer worked and a market economy that did not yet exist.

Two-Term Kuchma: The System Sinks Roots

Elections in new nations, while often eagerly anticipated, can produce unrest, even bloodletting. Ukraine's first presidential vote in 1994 was a welcome exception to this trend. Because no candidate won a majority in the first round, the two top contenders, Kravchuk and Leonid Kuchma, entered a runoff. Kuchma won with 52 percent to Kravchuk's 45 percent. Though the presidency changed hands peacefully, the elections revealed anew Ukraine's east-west division: Kravchuk, who billed himself as the guardian of independence and suggested that Kuchma would coddle Russia, carried the central provinces and dominated the western ones while Kuchma, who favored increased cooperation with Russia and official status for the Russian language, won almost three-fourths of the votes cast in the south and east.[35] Kuchma was reelected in 1999, defeating the communist party's candidate, Petro Symonenko. The regional divide appeared again: Kuchma, who stressed reform, won handily in the west, where Symonenko, aptly seen as a Soviet era relic and champion of integration with Russia, had scant support.

Unlike Kravchuk, Kuchma, who had served as prime minister from October 1992 to September 1993, was an easterner. Born in Chernihiv province and educated in Dnipropetrovs'k, he had made his career in the city's massive Yuzhmash complex, which produced ballistic missiles and rockets, and become its director. Despite Kuchma's background, his electoral base in the first election, and a campaign that played to eastern apprehensions about Ukrainianization were Kravchuk reelected, Ukraine's 1996 constitution did not provide for dual citizenship, Russian as a state language, or federalization. Nor did Kuchma support Crimean separatism.[36] Although the province had established a presidency and parliament in 1994, he eased out its pro-independence president in 1996 and abolished the office. The Crimean constitution adopted that year provided for autonomy but not separation.

Kuchma also contained the Crimean problem through the 1997 agreement with Russia on the Black Sea Fleet's status.[37] The fleet's ships were divided, with Russia getting over 82 percent of the ships and a twenty-year lease on Sevastopol with the possibility of a five-year extension. Ukraine received an annual rent of $97.75 million, to be applied against its $3 billion debt to Russia, and Moscow's recognition of Ukrainian sovereignty over Sevastopol. The deal would not prevent Crimea's separatists from seeking Moscow's support or from receiving encouragement from Russian nationalists, but it settled an unresolved issue that could have compounded Kyiv's Crimea problem. Still, in western Ukraine Kuchma was perceived as the representative of eastern powerbrokers favoring alignment with Russia.[38]

Although Kuchma stressed strengthening ties with Russia in his first campaign, he courted the EU and NATO and parried Russia's efforts to press Ukraine to strengthen ties with the CIS and to join the Collective Security Treaty Organization and the Eurasian Economic Community (EEC). He exchanged visits with U.S. President Bill Clinton and, together with Vice President Al Gore, chaired a commission created to expand cooperation between the United States and Ukraine. Ukraine also became the third largest recipient of American economic aid. In 1997, NATO and Ukraine signed a Charter on a Distinctive Partnership and in 2002 an Action Plan affirming Ukraine's "long-term goal of NATO membership."[39] In May 2002, Kuchma announced Ukraine's desire to join NATO, reaffirming it first in a presidential decree in July and later in Ukraine's June 2003 military doctrine, which committed Ukraine to becoming a "full-fledged member" of NATO and the EU. Kuchma's policy went beyond phraseology: Ukraine joined NATO's Partnership for Peace and held military maneuvers with NATO, and its troops supported the alliance's missions in Kosovo and Iraq. Kuchma was no less assiduous in pursuing integration with the EU, while realizing that membership remained a distant prospect.

Only when it was evident that neither western organization was about to offer Ukraine membership, or even a clear path to it, and that scandals produced by corruption, election rigging, and repression had undermined him in the West, did Kuchma tack toward Russia. In June 2004, he stated that Ukraine was not yet ready to join NATO, and a July presidential decree deleted the reference to NATO membership from Ukraine's military doctrine, substituting it with a reference to "a substantial deepening of relations with the alliance," a move that coincided with his meeting with Putin.[40] Having initially spurned the Russia-led EEC, Kuchma opened negotiations on membership in 2002; in 2003, he accepted the largely symbolic post of chairman of the CIS, whose plans for integration he had originally parried as part of the GUUAM coalition of Georgia, Ukraine, Uzbekistan, Azerbaijan, and Moldova.[41] His opponents' criticisms notwithstanding, these gestures were a far cry from integration with Russia.

As for Kuchma's domestic policies, it was during his two-term presidency that the worst features of Ukraine's political economy were established.[42] Still, the economic reforms of his first term, and the gains they brought, were undeniable. In 1996, a national currency, the hryvnia, replaced the stopgap karbovanets. Prices were decontrolled, and formerly scarce basic goods started reappearing on store shelves. Public expenditures were curbed. Inflation, which exceeded 400 percent in 1994, dipped to single digits by 1997. Export quotas and licenses that impeded efficiencies and ensured windfalls to crooked officials were cut back. Failing state companies that drained the treasury were privatized. Small enterprises were almost fully privatized by the end of 1996. Whereas 400 medium and large state enterprises had been sold by 1992, over 6,000 had been sold by early 1997. In 1992, the private sector accounted for about 10 percent of

GDP; by 2002, it accounted for 60 percent. Viktor Yushchenko, the respected former central bank chief, was appointed prime minister in December 1999, and though his tenure was short-lived (he was fired in May 2001), his reform program produced economic growth for the first time since independence, with the pickup commencing in 2000 and the pace averaging 8.4 percent through 2004.[43]

The reforms and growth rates drew praise from the West and from the IMF, which in 1994 and 1995 had supported Kuchma's reforms with loans totaling $2.5 billion. But the reforms of his first term stalled and became sporadic at best in the second. In part, that was because Kuchma himself was ambivalent about them. Moreover, seven different prime ministers served him, and the revolving door made for inconsistency and lack of follow-through. Then there was the resistance from the Rada's leftist parties and from wealthy and powerful vested interests. This constant pushback undid both Yushchenko and Yulia Tymoshenko, his deputy prime minister for energy. The pair initiated major changes that included closing tax loopholes benefitting the super-rich, ending secretive privatization schemes and the plum privileges of tycoons and their mega-companies, and attacking the corruption rampant in the gas distribution system. But Yushchenko's appointment had been a panic-induced last-ditch move to avert economic disaster. The reforms he and Tymoshenko pushed through had pinched the oligarchs and were anathema to the Rada's leftist parties. Both officials were soon fired: Yushchenko lasted a year and a half, Tymoshenko even less. By 2001 reform had run aground and problems mounted. Ukraine's unpaid energy bills to Russia totaled $4 billion, currency reserves had all but evaporated, creditors were being repaid through bond issues bearing sky-high interest rates, and Ukraine lingered on the edge of default.

Kuchma's privatization program degenerated into secretive and rigged fire sales of steel mills, coal mines, utilities, and television stations to the government's oligarchic allies. The big oligarchical clans were enriched; some were based in Kyiv, but most were in Donetsk and Dnipropetrovs'k, the stamping grounds of many top officials, Kuchma included. Corruption became colossal—not only because of piracy privatization but also because tax authorities and myriad regulators raked in bribes. Companies owned by oligarchs or managed by the allies of officials cornered the distribution of natural gas imports from Russia and Turkmenistan and used labyrinthine scams to dodge taxes and pile up huge profits. Unsurprisingly, domestic investment all but dried up, and there was little from abroad: the cronyism, corruption, and financial mess deterred foreign investors, who instead chose Eastern Europe, where reforms had produced growth and good governance.

A prime example of official corruption was Pavlo Lazarenko, prime minister in 1996–1997. He acquired a fortune worth tens of millions of dollars, aided by ill-gotten gains from an energy company to which he remained connected and by kickbacks passed on by regulators whom he oversaw. (Lazarenko would eventually be jailed in the United States for money laundering.) The privatization of the massive Krivorizhstal steel complex was another example. Despite higher bids, it was sold in 2004 for only $850 million to two oligarchs, Rinat Akhmetov, Ukraine's richest man, and Viktor Pinchuk, Kuchma's son-in-law.[44] (In 2005, Yushchenko, Kuchma's successor as president, nullified the deal, selling the conglomerate to Mittal Steel for $4.8 billion.) These were but two examples of runaway corruption.[45]

Naturally, the magnates were determined to maintain their privileges and favored access to government. The alluringly named political parties (Party of Greens of Ukraine, Labor Ukraine, and Social Democratic Party-United) they created served in practice as lobbies for their business interests, and they bankrolled Kuchma's second presidential campaign, during which their television networks lavished the incumbent with conspicuous, fawning coverage.[46]

It was hardly surprising that polls showed that most Ukrainians felt powerless and alienated from a state they considered corrupt, ineffective, and callous.[47] And the more unpopular the government became, the more it resorted to surveillance against its enemies, real or imagined.[48] Press freedoms declined as the state manipulated private mass media companies to its advantage, helped by the fact that the president's allies or relatives owned some of them.[49] Fearless investigative reporters risked harassment and intimidation. One persistent critic, the journalist Georgi Gongadze, suffered a worse fate: he disappeared in September 2000, only for his headless corpse to be discovered in November. Kuchma was soon embroiled in the resulting scandal when, in a secret tape recording made by his bodyguard (possibly at the behest of the Russian or Ukrainian intelligence services), the president, apparently in conversation with the interior minister, was heard suborning Gongadze's kidnapping.[50] The government denounced the tapes as doctored. Kuchma was never charged. But his political standing was shattered.

The Orange Revolution: Hope Unrequited

By 2002, change was in the air. Supporters of democracy and reform were hopeful, foes of change and beneficiaries of corruption apprehensive. Ahead of the upcoming Rada elections, Yushchenko and Tymoshenko had formed opposition parties. [51] His was Our Ukraine, with roots in the now dissipated Rukh, hers the Yulia Tymoshenko Bloc, consisting of her Fatherland Party and six others. Together with the Socialist Party, they constituted the reform forces. The forces of the establishment were the Social Democratic Party-United and Kuchma's For a United Ukraine coalition, a composite of three parties formed by powerful eastern clans. The reformers made a strong showing: Yushchenko's party won 118 seats and nearly 24 percent of the vote. As in the 1998 elections, half the deputies hailed from single-member constituencies based on a simple majority, half from ones in which parties received seats based on their proportion of the vote—an arrangement that enabled the government to prevent a reform-minded majority. With some exceptions, the parties of Yushchenko and Tymoshenko fared well in central and western areas and poorly in the south and east, where the communists and the establishment dominated. [52]

The 2002 legislative election was a bellwether for the 2004 presidential vote. Shaken by Yushchenko's success, the government and its allies maneuvered to thwart his bid for the presidency and to reduce his power should he prevail. [53] One ploy was the abortive effort to exempt Kuchma from the constitutional ban on third terms, on the grounds that the Constitution was adopted two years after he was first elected. A second, successful scheme involved strengthening the position of prime minister, then held by Viktor Yanukovych, the Donbas oligarchs' man. A third ploy involved orchestrating a Yanukovych candidacy and victory. The fourth, and most egregious, was the failed poisoning of Yushchenko in the summer of 2004, which boosted his popularity and further discredited the government.

Following blatant vote rigging connived by a partisan election commission, Yanukovych was declared the winner of the November runoff. Irate crowds massed in Kyiv. The city's Independence Square ("Maidan") was awash in orange, the color symbolizing Yushchenko's party. Tent cities sprung up as protestors kept vigil around the clock. Tymoshenko's oratory revved up the throngs. On the other side, the head of Yanukovych's party held a referendum on the creation of a "south-eastern state" were Yushchenko to become president, while the council of Donetsk province voted to hold a referendum on whether the region should become a republic.[54] After prolonged backroom negotiations, mediated by the EU and held amidst the unrelenting protests and splits within the power structure, the government caved. A new election was held in December. Yushchenko won, 51.2 percent to Yanukovych's 44.2 percent. As in the previous runoff, he dominated the center and west, Yanukovych the east and south.

Yushchenko was an ethnic Ukrainian, and, though not a westerner (he was born in the northern province of Sumy), he was viewed in the Russophone regions as an advocate of Ukrainianization and integration with the West at Russia's expense. The east-west divide appeared once again. As one account put it: "While Yushchenko's voters celebrated in Kiev and the West, a wave of rallies rolled through Yanukovych strongholds in the east to protest what people there saw as a stolen election. Defiant of Kiev's authority, politicians in the east angrily rejected the decision to call another poll, with some calling for federalization and even the creation of a new autonomous region. Others went further and threatened to merge eastern Ukraine with Russia."[55] Based on surveys, Mark Beissinger found that the Orange protestors "were eight times more likely to be from Western Ukraine," while their opponents "were three times more likely to speak Russian at home and . . . six times more likely to be from a single province of Ukraine (Donetsk—the province of Yanukovych's political base) than the rest of the adult population of Ukraine."[56]

There was another east-west aspect to the revolution, and it was international. Western governments, though circumspect in public, backed the Orange movement—just as they had the earlier Rose Revolution in Georgia in 2003. A flood of western NGOs did too. Yanukovych, his entourage, and the pro-regime media railed against this "foreign interference" even though they were beneficiaries of Russian backing. Convinced that the West had orchestrated Georgia's upheaval, Moscow was determined to avert a Ukrainian version. Moscow decried Western interference but did not disguise its own backing of Yanukovych, which even Russian scholars characterized as "conspicuous and crude."[57] Putin visited Kyiv several times in 2004 to show his support for Yanukovych, who was advised by Russian political operatives and joined on the campaign trail by Moscow's nationalist mayor Yuri Luzhkov.[58] Even the Russian Orthodox Church weighed in for Yanukovych, as did its local affiliate, the Ukrainian Orthodox Church (Moscow Patriarchate).[59]

The Orange Revolution raised hopes only to prove a crashing disappointment. Ukrainians soon realized that the old system and its pathologies had survived, albeit with a new crew: as early as November 2005, almost 60 percent opined in a survey that the country was on the wrong track.[60] What happened? To begin with, the revolution's prime movers proved a disastrous duo as rulers. Yushchenko picked the flamboyant Tymoshenko as prime minister but soon moved to clip her wings. He appointed the billionaire confectionary magnate Petro Poroshenko as head of the National Security Council to serve as a counterbalance, and the infighting between Tymoshenko and Poroshenko, who established something akin to a parallel government, was poisonous. Yushchenko either could not or would not stop it and looked like the weak head of a house divided. Worse, his antipathy toward Tymoshenko bordered on obsession.

Tymoshenko was fired in September 2005, along with the rest of a fractious government, and went into opposition, charging Yushchenko with having "practically ruined our unity, our future, the future of the country."[61] The hostility between the two ran so deep that, following the 2006 Rada elections, Yushchenko's Our Ukraine eschewed a majority coalition with Tymoshenko's party and the Socialists and instead cut a deal with the Yanukovych's Party of Regions that enabled him to become prime minister in August. Yanukovych promptly employed his new post to weaken Yushchenko. Tymoshenko returned as prime minister after the 2007 Rada elections, in which her party did even better, while Our Ukraine and the Party of Regions lost ground. Yet the Yushchenko-Tymoshenko duel dragged on, destroying the unity that sustained the revolution.

Personality differences were not the only problem. As part of the deal he made with the Kuchma regime in the aftermath of the Orange Revolution, Yushchenko had to accept a constitution that weakened the presidency while strengthening the Rada and the prime minister. This created a structural basis for hostility between president and prime minister. Then there were the incessant battles between the president and the parliament, which became particularly destructive in the absence of a stable Rada majority. Fractiousness was pervasive, as were personal vendettas, ideological squabbles, and defections. Yanukovych and the Party of Regions added to the instability by hyping the east vs. west divide: no matter the issue, they invariably framed it as an instance of abiding east-west differences over language, regional autonomy, and Russia.

Then there was the continuing corruption, which reached into the government's upper ranks and even the president's family.[62] Yushchenko's chief of staff and some ministers retained ties to businesses in energy, banking, and telecommunication and even received payments from those they regulated. The super-rich continued to profit from shady deals. An example was RosUkrEnergo, designated in a 2006 agreement between prime ministers Putin and Tymoshenko as the middleman for Ukraine's gas imports. Owned by Gazprom and the Ukrainian oligarch Dmytro Firtash, the company's opacity and profit skimming made it a byword for corruption. The president's own reputation was tarnished by his brother's use of political connections to amass wealth and by his son's lavish lifestyle. Tymoshenko, known as the "gas princess" for having allegedly accumulated millions of dollars illicitly while working in the energy trade with the disgraced ex-Prime Minister Lazarenko (before he headed the government), was making her own back-room deals with tycoons.

The political disarray and corruption increased the oligarchs' power.[63] They continued creating factions within the major political parties and forming additional parties as fronts. Akhmetov, the Donetsk billionaire and Yanukovych supporter, had a phalanx in the Rada delegation of the Party of Regions. Other tycoons and companies backed Yushchenko's and Tymoshenko's parties. Principles perished, opportunism reigned. Poroshenko, among the founders of the Party of Regions in 2001, later financed Yushchenko's election campaign and then entered his government. (He would later join the government of Yushchenko's archrival, Yanukovych, serving in 2012 under Prime Minister Mykola Azarov as Minister for Trade and Economic Development.) Big businesses that backed Tymoshenko's party seamlessly became patrons of Yushchenko's. The parasitic partnership between the oligarchs and the state reconfirmed Ukrainians' conviction that politics amounted to bribes and backroom deals among indistinguishable political and economic elites.

Yushchenko struggled to build the consensus for a clear economic policy. Goaded by the IMF, which pledged $16.5 billion in loans, his government moved to reduce budget deficits by hiking gas and electricity prices and pruning social services. But he faced pressure, from within his administration and from the parliamentary opposition, to increase wages and pensions and to provide aid to local governments, especially as the economy slowed. The result: inflation reached 12.3 percent in 2004, climbing to 16.6 percent in 2006, and fell only after growth plunged as the waves of the 2008 financial crisis reached Ukraine.[64] Although economic growth exceeded 7 percent in 2006 and reached nearly 8 percent in 2007, it fell to 2 percent in 2008. GDP contracted by nearly 15 percent in 2009 before growth revived to 4 percent in 2010.[65] Unemployment, 6.8 percent in 2006, edged close to 9 percent in 2009 and still stood at 8 percent in 2010.[66] Real wages increased between 2004 and 2006, but fell steeply as the economy slowed. Public debt rose from 15.9 percent of GDP in 2006 to 37.7 percent in 2010.[67] Besides sullying politics, corruption hindered growth by scaring investors. If corruption was bad under Kuchma, it became worse under Yushchenko: in Transparency International's corruption ranking, Ukraine moved from 122nd place in 2004 to 146th in 2009, on par with Zimbabwe.[68]

Yushchenko's first official trip abroad, barely a day after he took office, was to Russia, and he would later withdraw the Ukrainian troops Kuchma had sent to Iraq to support NATO. Yet these moves did not reassure Russia, for two reasons. First, the new president made it clear that his priority was integrating with EU and NATO, which to Moscow meant Ukraine's impending turn away from Russia. Yushchenko's conduct during the August 2008 Russia-Georgia war served to confirm this suspicion. He rushed to Tbilisi with the leaders of Poland and the Baltic states, which Moscow considered NATO's anti-Russia quartet. In a *Washington Post* op-ed he declared that Ukraine "has become a hostage in the war waged by Russia," condemned the "looting and destruction" of Georgia, proposed a UN peacekeeping force, and offered to provide Ukrainian troops.[69] Because Russia's Black Sea Fleet participated in the war, he issued decrees—ignored by Russia, criticized by Tymoshenko as provocative—requiring that it obtain Kyiv's permission before exiting and entering Sevastopol.[70] In December 2008, Ukraine and the United States signed a Charter on Strategic Partnership providing for "cooperation across a broad spectrum of mutual priorities" based on "shared values and interests," including "protecting security and territorial integrity."[71]

Most Ukrainians did not share Yushchenko's enthusiasm for NATO membership—a long shot at best—and Ukraine's constitution forbade foreign military bases. But neither fact reassured Moscow. After all, a loophole had been found for its own Black Sea Fleet's base in Sevastopol, and Kuchma had shown that there was abundant scope for cooperating with NATO short of joining it; his decrees and the 2003 changes to Ukraine's military doctrine had demonstrated that the constitutional provision prohibiting foreign bases could be parsed to permit participation in military pacts. Nor did the Kremlin consider Ukraine's integration with Europe as purely commercial given the security structures associated with the EU's Common Security and Defense Policy. Besides, the EU and NATO had overlapping membership and had been steadily expanding eastwards. Moscow regarded membership in the former as a pathway to the latter.

The second and arguably more important reason was that Yushchenko's political base was in western and central Ukraine, areas the Kremlin considered, not unfairly, the citadels of pro-western and anti-Russia sentiment. While Yushchenko was not from the West, Moscow regarded him a fervent nationalist. Whatever Kuchma's dealings with the West, his ties to Russophone Ukraine had reassured Russia, as did his gestures toward the CIS and the Eurasian Economic Community and his backtracking on NATO. Yushchenko, in contrast, moved to commemorate the 75th anniversary of the Holodomor, which he described as a "state-organized program of mass starvation" that had killed "an estimated seven million to ten million Ukrainians, including up to a third of the nation's children" and amounted to genocide.[72] Though built on the earlier pronouncements of Kuchma and Yanukovich, as well as on a 2006 parliamentary resolution that had described the famine in similar terms, Yushchenko's statement was denounced, by both the Party of Regions and Russian leaders, as an example of chauvinism, revisionism, and anti-Russian animus. Russian President Dmitry Medvedev wrote Yushchenko directly, accusing him of falsifying the historical record and making the "so-called Holodomor" and the pursuit of a Membership Action Plan in NATO "a central element of Ukrainian foreign policy." The Russian leadership's anger mounted when the Yushchenko government sought to get the

UN General Assembly to recognize the famine as a genocide and to hold Russian leaders of the time legally accountable.[73]

Arguably more controversial was Yushchenko's designation of two wartime nationalist leaders, Roman Shukhevych (who had commanded the UPA) and Stepan Bandera, as Heroes of Ukraine. Somewhat less controversial was Yushchenko's commissioning of a monument, and the renaming of a street, honoring Hetman Ivan Mazepa, the Cossack leader who fought with Sweden's King Charles XII against Russia at the Battle of Poltava in 1709.[74] Anathematized ever since by the Russian Orthodox Church, branded a reactionary during the Soviet times, the Hetman is reviled in standard Russian historiography and symbolizes treachery to many Russophone Ukrainians, enough to foment protests over Yushchenko's decision. Yushchenko also rebuffed Putin's proposal for a joint celebration of the battle's 300th anniversary, proposing instead to join the Swedish government to mark the tercentenary of the partnership between Sweden and Ukraine.[75] (The Russian ambassador to Ukraine, and a former Prime Minister under Yeltsin, Viktor Chernomyrdin, remarked hyperbolically that building a Mazepa monument at Poltava was comparable to erecting a statue of Hitler at Stalingrad.)[76] For many Russians, Mazepa betrayed the Eastern Slavs' unity; for many Ukrainians, he resisted imperial Russia. Once again, a historical legacy poisoned present-day politics.[77]

Gas Wars with Russia

Russia had means to register its displeasure over Ukraine's post-Orange Revolution policies, and energy was the most powerful one. Dating from Soviet times, Ukraine and other Soviet republics had received Russian gas at heavily discounted prices, and

this concessional arrangement continued after 1991. Access
to cheap gas meant that Ukraine faced no pressure to fix its
immensely inefficient energy use, and with Gazprom's forbear-
ance its unpaid bills piled up. By 2008, Ukraine was importing
56 billion cubic meters (bcm) from Russia annually, the bulk
of its consumption. Meanwhile, the difference between the
prices it paid and those Europe paid on average had more than
doubled, and oil prices, to which gas prices were indexed, had
soared. Russia pressed its CIS customers to pay more, though it
offered discounts to friendly states (Armenia and Belarus), especially if they would swap their gas debts for Russian equity in
their pipelines and storage facilities. But Yushchenko's Ukraine
wasn't deemed friendly by Moscow and would not sell its energy
facilities. Soon, Kyiv and Moscow were jousting over gas prices,

Figure 1.3
Major natural gas pipelines in Ukraine.

and because 80 percent of Russia's European gas exports flowed through Ukraine's pipeline network, Europe was soon dragged into the tussle. (See Figure 1.3.)

The first tiff occurred in 2006, triggered by Russia's demand for an increase from $50 per thousand cubic meters to $230.[78] Ukraine refused to pay. Russia cut off supplies, and flows to Europe fell. Russia accused Kyiv of "stealing" gas designated for Europe; Ukraine responded that it had bought the gas in question from Turkmenistan. The dispute's effects on Europe were minimal, and a three-year agreement was soon reached at a price of $95. RosUkrEnergo became the latest middleman, buying gas from Turkmenistan and Russia and selling to Ukraine's state-owned company, Naftohaz—a windfall for the Ukrainian oligarch, Firtash, whose stake in RosUkrEnergo was 45 percent. (Gazprom's was 50 percent.)

The 2009 dispute, by contrast, spawned a crisis. In another example of their fratricidal duels, Yushchenko rejected a December 2008 deal that Tymoshenko, back for her second stint as prime minister, had reached with Putin, then Russia's prime minister. That left Ukraine and Russia without a new contract on gas prices and transit fees. Russia demanded a price hike, first to $250 per thousand cubic meters, then to $450. Ukraine balked. On January 1, Russia cut the volume designated for Ukraine but continued shipments earmarked for Europe and again accused Ukraine of pilfering Europe's gas. Ukraine responded that absent a contract it was entitled to the gas in its pipeline system. Within days, Russia's gas flows to Europe ceased in what was a chilly winter.

Frenzied negotiations yielded a ten-year agreement between Putin and Tymoshenko on January 19, 2009, ending the crisis.[79] But the terms ensured that there would be another conflict before long. The deal guaranteed Ukraine 52 bcm of gas per year in 2009–2019, but it was required to buy that volume regardless of need, and if it required more, there would be a hefty markup. The price for 2009 was fixed at 80 percent of the European average, more than three times what Ukraine paid under the 2006 accord. And it would reach the European level between 2009–2019 and be indexed quarterly to oil prices. Ukraine's era of cut-rate prices was over. This meant that Ukraine would struggle to pay its gas bills on time—unless Gazprom was charitable. Gazprom was not, however, a free agent: the Russian government had a controlling share, and Moscow's handling of Ukraine's debts would not hinge on financial considerations alone but on its assessment of Ukraine's internal and external policies as well, and perhaps more so.

Yanukovych's Thermidor: the Road to Crisis

As the January 2010 presidential election approached, Yushchenko and his party had lost their luster. The economy was in the doldrums, the parliament remained a battleground, and the Yushchenko-Tymoshenko feud flared on. For many Ukrainians the Orange Revolution had been betrayed. Yushchenko was eliminated in the first round of the election after winning a mere 5.5 percent of the vote, placing fifth, and passing the 1 percent mark in only one province, Lviv.[80] Yanukovych won 35 percent of the vote, Tymoshenko 25 percent, and in the runoff held in February, he won 49 percent to her 45.5 percent. Her best showing was in the center and west, his in the south and east, where he took 77 percent of the vote compared to 18 percent in the central and western provinces.[81]

The new president, who was cut from different cloth than Yushchenko and Tymoshenko, owed his stunning comeback less to his political and intellectual stature than to Yushchenko's failures.[82] Born in a village in Donetsk, of which province he was governor from 1997 to 2002, he was uncharismatic and poorly educated, despite the equivalent of a Ph.D. in economics from a fly-by-night university, and had been jailed in his youth for robbery and assault.

He relied overwhelmingly on Russophone Ukraine for political support and had long favored alignment with Russia and official status for the Russian language. Moscow hailed his election—and had reason to be pleased. Yanukovych backed away from his position on the 1932–1933 famine, declaring in remarks to the Parliamentary Assembly of the Council of Europe in April 2010 that it had not, in fact, been a case of genocide and that labeling it as such was "incorrect and unjust."[83] And in another move that pleased Moscow, in June he signed legislation he had submitted to parliament declaring Ukraine a non-aligned country, thus effectively ruling out NATO membership.[84]

In much of the rest of Ukraine his background, career, and political views aroused suspicion. One example on the cultural front was the uproar that followed the Rada's adoption in July 2012 of a new language law that Yanukovych signed in August. It preserved Ukrainian's position as the state language but permitted city and regional authorities to declare Russian the official language if at least 10 percent of the inhabitants deemed it their native tongue. The law was controversial because Russian was already the de facto language of official and public use in most of southern and eastern Ukraine. As such, it did not fall under the category of a "minority language" that needed state protection. Ukrainophone Ukrainians therefore feared that the law would enable pro-Russian forces to roll back the gains made by Ukrainian in schools and the media. They saw the legislation as a brazen attempt to diminish Ukrainian's status as the state language—making it a mere formality—and to preserve Russian's traditional dominance. The language law turned explosive: protests erupted in the Rada, and the Kyiv police used truncheons and tear gas against demonstrators.[85]

Table 1.1 shows that the new legislation would have applied to 11 provinces along with Kyiv. Apart from Kyiv and the Chernihiv and Sumy provinces, the rest are in Ukraine's south and east.

Although the law's provision also applied to other minority languages, both its supporters and detractors knew that its goal was to enhance the status of Russian. The law's effect, in short, was to pit supporters of Ukraine's two main language groups against each other. In the south and east, and particularly in

Ukrainian Provinces with At Least Ten Percent of Residents Identifying Russian as First Language	
Province	Percentage
Crimea	76.6
Donetsk	74.9
Luhansk	68.6
Zaporizhia	48.0
Odessa	42.0
Dnipropetrovs'k	31.9
Mykolaiv	29.3
Kyiv City	25.0
Kherson	24.9
Sumy	15.5
Chernihiv	10.3

Table 1.1

Ukrainian provinces with at least ten percent of residents identifying Russian as first language. Source: Radio Free Europe/Radio Liberty, Auguest 25, 2014; http://www.rferl.org/contentinfographics/map-ukraine-percentage-who-identify-as-ethnic-russians-or-say-russian-is-their-first-language-/25323841.html.

Crimea and the Donbas, agitation for raising Russian's official status had a long history, so the law was acclaimed, with several cities and provinces implementing it straightaway.[86] In the center and west, where the percentage of those who regard Russian as their first language was in the single digits, the reaction was different.[87]

On the political front, the Yanukovych regime soon became emblematic of sleaze. The reputation was deserved, no matter that the corrupt practices under Yanukovych were exaggerated manifestations of patterns prevalent under Ukraine's prior governments. Ultimately, pervasive corruption was the product of a resilient system of political economy—one that transcended leaders and governments and was defended by vested interests that gained power and wealth from its persistence. Capturing and retaining control of the state therefore became a battle for big stakes in which few holds were barred. Few of the schemes carried out under Yanukovych were new; what was different was the scale of corruption and the blitheness with which it was practiced.[88] Symbolic of the regime's excesses was Yanukovych's palatial residence north of Kyiv, "Mezhyhirya," adorned, at enormous state expense, with lavish—and remarkably tasteless—decorations. By 2012–2013, Ukrainians openly spoke of the Yanukovych Family, a small coterie of cronies cozy with the president and his dentist-turned-billionaire banker son, Oleksandr, who reportedly took a hefty cut of any large deal in Ukraine.

The corruption had wide effects. The super-wealthy and politically powerful fought over the distribution of wealth and influence, while small and medium-sized businesses atrophied. Prosecutors, tax authorities, and courts were used to hound political opponents. Independent-minded journalists were intimidated through such measures as the 2012 amendments to the Criminal Code that narrowed the definition of slander and provided for fines and imprisonment.[89] Pro-government tycoons used their television networks and newspapers for parochial political ends, notably during elections. Donbas elites raided the Kyiv real estate market and bought up or extorted plum properties at cut-rate prices. Oligarchs deployed their wealth to cajole the president, cabinet, and legislature to win pecuniary privileges and to keep those they already had. The families and allies of top officials, particularly the president's, accumulated wealth and stashed it in foreign tax havens. In Transparency International's corruption index Ukraine ranked 144th in 2013, on par with Nigeria.[90]

Moreover, corruption created a continuing inducement for perpetuating the maze of regulations, permits, licenses, and rigged privatizations. A massive and intrusive state bureaucracy provided political power and myriad means for building patronage networks. Consider a typical example. Ukrtelecom, a monopolistic state-owned telecommunications firm, was sold to a single bidder; ten other companies were banned from competing.[91] The winning firm was registered abroad, the identity of its owners never disclosed. Such practices help explain how Yanukovych lived opulently and how he and his family amassed billions of dollars. None of this was a secret; Yanukovych himself boasted about the scale of corruption.[92] A ruling elite that could rake in billons of dollars by favoring friends and extracting kickbacks for essential transactions could have no commitment to transparency and competition, no matter what it told the IMF, the World Bank, and the EU. Nor would the oligarchs who thrived under such a system, despite hopes in some quarters that they would metamorphose into good capitalists, favor clean governance.

Emblematic of Yanukovich's indifference to rule of law was the jailing of Yulia Tymoshenko. The charges against her, widely viewed as politically motivated, led to kangaroo court proceedings that culminated in a seven-year sentence in 2011. She was charged with a litany of illegalities: bribery, overstepping her authority as prime minister in reaching the 2009 gas contract with Putin, fraud while working in the gas trade with Lazarenko during the 1990s, and even complicity in murder. Although Tymoshenko was a controversial figure, imprisonment made her a martyr and a symbol of the regime's venality and viciousness. She became an icon in international human rights circles, and the EU made her release a condition for the ratification of the Association Agreement with Ukraine. Yet the more the unpopular his government became, the more determined Yanukovych was to keep her confined. Tymoshenko's wide following, electric persona, and rousing oratory—all displayed during the Orange Revolution—made her the one figure capable of defeating him in the 2016 presidential election. And defeat would mean not just the loss of power and wealth for him and his allies but probably judicial proceedings and imprisonment as well. So the stakes were high.

On the economic front, Yanukovych began his presidency by promising Ukrainians that they would soon live in a prosperous country that would be a center of global business. Helped by influential international experts, his administration unveiled a program for 2010–2014 entitled "Prosperous Society, Competitive Economic, Effective State."[93] But he wound up producing neither prosperity nor a business-friendly environment.

In 1989, Ukraine's GDP per capita exceeded Russia's; in 2012 it amounted to 25 percent of Russia's.[94] In the World

Bank's 2013 per capita national income rankings, which are based on purchasing power parity, Ukraine's $8,960 ranked 127th out of 213 countries, barely ahead of Kosovo. Only six other ex-Soviet states—Armenia, Georgia, Uzbekistan, Moldova, Kyrgyzstan, and Tajikistan—trailed it.[95] Economic growth recovered after 2009, reaching 4.2 percent in 2010 and 5.2 percent in 2011, but plunged to 0.2 percent in 2012 and 1.9 percent in 2013. [96] The government's much-touted anti-corruption program was a "total failure," according to commentators, and Ukraine remained "among the worst in Europe" as a business venue.[97]

Despite pressure from the IMF, the fear of a popular backlash prevented the reduction of state expenditures.[98] Yanukovych's government backed such budget cutting measures as eliminating energy subsidies, cutting social services, delaying the retirement age, and reducing pensions. But these measures could not be reconciled with the supreme imperative of winning elections and preventing rebellions. So they were watered down, enacted in part, or simply not at all.[99] Consequently, the revenue-spending gap persisted, reducing the confidence of domestic and foreign businesses and, in turn, inhibiting investment and diminishing job creation, competition, and tax revenues.

The failure to cut energy subsidies substantially also meant that state expenditures increased because gas prices did. The Putin-Tymoshenko gas agreement was indexed to oil prices. Inevitably, as oil prices rose, Ukraine's energy bill increased, while energy efficiency did not.[100] Naftohaz's mounting arrears became the government's responsibility, adding to budget deficits and boosting borrowing—at high rates because skittish lenders demanded premiums. Yanukovych tried to escape this trap by signing the July 2010 Kharkiv Accords with Russia that extended the Black Sea Fleet's lease on Sevastopol from 2017 to 2042 in return for cheaper gas. But the new price was substantially higher than what Ukraine had paid before 2009 and in any event remained tied to oil prices.[101]

The system of vast corruption explains in part why Yanukovych eventually shelved the Association Agreement (AA) and the Deep and Comprehensive Free Trade Area (DCFTA) accord after a long dalliance. The negotiations had been underway since March 2007, and the accords were finally initialed in March 2012. But signature and ratification was held up on the European side by doubts about whether Yanukovych would implement the avalanche of mandated economic and political reforms.[102] Moreover, the EU insisted on Tymoshenko's release. But radical reforms were incompatible with the survival of the system that amounted to a cash cow for Yanukovych and the lobbies backing him. And freeing Tymoshenko would have put his political future at risk.

The Kremlin remained wary of Ukraine's integration with Europe and opposed the AA. Instead, it pressed Yanukovych to join the Russia-Belarus-Kazakhstan Customs Union. Russia, with its massive energy stocks and financial reserves, enticed Ukraine with a $15 billion loan and a 25 percent cut in gas prices once Yanukovych put the AA/DCFTA on ice in November 2013. But Russian pressure or rewards alone were not decisive because Ukraine would have gained a great deal from the AA, including access to a European market of 753 million consumers, foreign investment, technology, and reduced Russian leverage. But implementing it would have dismantled the system that provided wealth and power to Yanukovych, the Party of Regions, and many powerful groups.

Yanukovych's turn away from the AA was thus above all an act of self- and system-preservation. The irony is that it ended up provoking a revolt that brought him and his government down. It also undid Russia's gains by reviving Ukraine's alignment with the West. That realignment, as we show in the next chapter, ignited the gravest crisis that has occurred between Russia and the West since the Cold War.

2 Nobody Expected a Crisis

The Ukraine crisis erupted with little warning and caught virtually everyone on both sides of the Atlantic—Kyiv, Brussels, Washington, and Moscow—off guard. But, as we showed in Chapter 1, the seeds of the crisis had been planted decades before, and it was only a matter of time before they would emerge and consume the country. Although few, if anyone, predicted the crisis, after its outbreak it appeared all but inevitable, fueled by various causes both at home and abroad.

This chapter offers an overview of the main stages of the crisis as it unfolded—from President Viktor Yanukovych's sudden withdrawal from negotiations with the European Union about an association agreement in November 2013, to September 2014, when the ceasefire agreed to by Moscow and Kyiv marked the end of the summer military campaign. This chapter will also look beyond the crisis itself to examine the key factors, both internal and external to Ukraine, that built up over a period of well over a decade and culminated in the fall of Yanukovych in February 2014.

The Domestic Setting

The three years of Viktor Yanukovych's presidency from 2010 to 2013 had been quite uneventful. The relative calm of those years stood in stark contrast to the political turbulence of the 2004–2005 Orange Revolution, when hundreds of thousands of ordinary Ukrainians took to the streets to protest the compromised presidential election. These protests propelled to power a team of reform-minded politicians who promised to restore democratic governance, clean up corruption, and forge close ties with the West. However, quickly mired in internecine squabbles and allegations of corruption, they were unable to deliver on their promises, and the five-year presidency of their leader Viktor Yushchenko proved a disappointment to the populace.[1] Ukrainians' disappointment with the reformers was so deep that in a 2010 presidential election generally considered free and fair, they chose Viktor Yanukovych, the loser of the 2005 presidential contest.[2]

Tired of Politics

Ukrainians seemed to have lost their revolutionary spirit and opted for promises of stability and managerial competence over change.[3] The country was sliding into political apathy. A late 2011 poll conducted by the International Republican Institute (IRI) showed little appetite on the part of the Ukrainian public for the kind of revolutionary activities that swept many parts of the country in 2004 and would re-appear in 2013. Fifty-five percent of those polled disapproved of protests without appropriate government permits, nearly 70 percent opposed blocking major roads, and 74 percent were against occupying buildings. Of the issues most worrisome to Ukrainians personally, the top three were high cost of living, unemployment, and social welfare.[4]

A strong sense of apathy and disillusionment with the country's political system and mistrust of political parties were also visible in the section of the poll dealing with political issues. By far the greatest number of respondents—41 percent—said that they would vote for a political party only if a "new political power" appeared on the scene. The second greatest number—27 percent—answered that nothing could make them vote for any political party. Sixty-three percent expected that the 2012 parliamentary election would not be free and fair.

Apathy and disillusionment with politics and politicians also manifested themselves in the Ukrainian public's reaction to the imprisonment and trial of Yanukovych's main rival in the 2010 presidential election and leader of the Orange Revolution, Yulia Tymoshenko. The trial of Tymoshenko, the face of the Orange Revolution who had mobilized and sustained the protest energy of hundreds of thousands of Ukrainians, triggered no mass protests, and only a few thousand supporters came to the courthouse to object to her trial and verdict.[5] Ukrainians were tired of politics.

Their disillusionment with the political process manifested itself again in the fall of 2012, when Ukraine elected a new parliament. The election, as expected by the majority of Ukrainians, was severely compromised and heavily criticized by the international community as well as by the leaders of the opposition parties in Ukraine.[6] Despite the relatively high turnout—58 percent—and the widely reported violations of the electoral laws, the election that gave a plurality of seats in the parliament to Yanukovych's Party of Regions (PoR) triggered only minor protests led by opposition politicians who claimed to have been defrauded by the government.[7] The Orange revolution had receded into the past.

Yanukovych Gathers Strength

Against this backdrop of political apathy and disillusionment, Yanukovych and his circle of associates, especially his family members, accumulated both political power and wealth.[8] The family's wealth was on public display following Yanukovych's sudden flight from Ukraine in February 2014, although rumors about his son Oleksandr's rapidly growing fortune had circulated well before that.

Looking toward his reelection campaign in 2015, Yanukovich pushed to ensure that his own clan or friendly interests controlled major media outlets. Since 95 percent of the population of Ukraine depends on television for political information, control of this medium was essential.[9] The president's associates and allies took over some television channels and pressured prominent Ukrainian businessmen who owned other channels and depended on the government's good will to keep their businesses.[10] In February 2013, Inter Media Group, including the country's most popular television channel, was sold to Dmyrto Firtash, a powerful billionaire gas trader with ties to the president. Inter's previous owner Valeriy Khoroshkovskiy reportedly had had a falling out with Yanukovych and his Prime Minister Mykola Azarov.[11] In June 2013, one of Ukraine's largest media conglomerates was sold to a little-known businessman reported to be acting as a front for the Yanukovych clan.[12]

Yanukovych also succeeded in placing his loyalists in key government posts to ensure his control of law enforcement, courts, the security apparatus, and financial flows. To the post of prosecutor general, he appointed Viktor Pshonka, who, after the overthrow of the Yanukovych government, gained notoriety for his lavish lifestyle. Other posts—head of the Security Service (SBU), Interior Ministry, and Constitutional Court—went to loyal Yanukovych supporters as well. A Yanukovych family insider Serhiy Arbuzov was appointed head of the Central Bank and, later, as first deputy prime minister.

Yanukovych also took full advantage of Ukraine's crony capitalist system. Yanukovych's relationship with the country's wealthiest oligarch, Rinat Akhmetov, reportedly predated his presidency. The two had roots in Donetsk, where Yanukovych had served as governor from 1997 to 2002 and Akhmetov began his business career.[13] Other oligarchs reported to have joined the president's camp and the government at one time or another include billionaire gas trader Dmytro Firtash, banker and Deputy Primer Minister Serhiy Tihipko, as well as other lesser-known figures. Even Ukraine's current president Petro Poroshenko served in Yanukovich's government.[14]

Yanukovych's relationship with Ukrainian oligarchs was hampered by the predatory nature of his own clan, whose members aggressively sought to expand their own political power and business interests at the expense of others.[15,16] This ruthless pursuit of power and money fueled frictions within the country's business and political elite and eventually contributed to Yanukovych's downfall.[17]

However, until the very end of Yanukovych's presidency few oligarchs dared to challenge the president openly, and those who did paid a price for it. Some—including the current governor of the Dnipropetrovsk region, Ihor Kolomoyskyi—resisted the pressure from the president's clan, while others, including former SBU chief and Inter TV owner Valeriy Khoro-shkovskiy, had to sell their media assets and flee Ukraine, reportedly fearing for their safety.[18]

Signs of Trouble to Come

With the public docile, the government and the media under his control, the financial resources at his disposal, Tymoshenko in prison, the opposition suffering from the legacy of the failed Orange Revolution and factional infighting, and the oligarchs cowed, Yanukovych looked unassailable. But looks were deceiving: the superficial calm of his secure position at the top of the power pyramid concealed signs of underlying weakness.

Public opinion data from the period of Yanukovych's presidency leave no doubt that, although apathetic, the people of Ukraine had few illusions about the nature of their president and the revolving door between his government and the business and political elite. Thanks in large part to Ukraine's relatively free—or free-for-all—media environment, which became an arena for competition between business groups with competing interests, the virtually unlimited sway that the moneyed interests held over Ukrainian politics and economy was clear enough. The majority of the public—71 percent—thought that the country was moving in the wrong direction, and only 13 percent said that it was moving in the right direction. "Corruption within the state bodies" was among the three most important problems in Ukraine, second only to unemployment.[19] The same data illustrated the low esteem in which the public held the country's political class: 27 percent replied that they would not vote for any existing political party in Ukraine, while 41 percent said that they would vote for a political party only if a new trustworthy party emerged.

The oligarchs, notwithstanding—or perhaps because of—their enormous wealth and influence over the nation's life, were hardly a trusted source of support for the Yanukovych regime. Having benefited hugely from the crony capitalist system that gave rise to Yanukovych, the oligarchs were vulnerable to his relentless pursuit of even more power and wealth. While undoubtedly keen to protect the system, they were also mindful that Yanukovych had the power to undercut their business interests and limit their power as a class.

Despite Yanukovych's efforts to establish a firm hold on the security and law enforcement agencies, their loyalty too was uncertain. While the top leadership that was hand-picked by Yanukovych and part of his inner circle could be relied on to support his regime in a crisis, the rank-and-file would be confronted with the dilemma that any authoritarian regime's security service confronts when ordered to move against its own people—to support the regime or side with the people. With the precedent of Ukraine's security service staying on the sidelines during the Orange revolution, and the nature of the Yanukovych regime transparent to the people of Ukraine, no one could or should have taken for granted the security personnel's loyalty to the president in a crisis.[20]

The opposition too was a significant factor in domestic politics—despite its lack of cohesion, the legacy of failed governance following the Orange Revolution, and pressure from the Yanukovych regime. Heavyweight boxing champion Vitaliy Klitschko's Ukrainian Democratic Alliance for Reform (UDAR) got 40 seats in the 2012 parliamentary election. Yulia Tymoshenko's Fatherland got 101 seats, and Oleh Tyahnybok's far-right

Freedom got 37 seats. These results enabled the opposition to remain an important voice in the country's political life.[21]

In short, despite Yanukovych's pursuit of dominance in Ukrainian domestic politics, the underlying conditions were nowhere as favorable as the relatively calm surface would lead one to believe. Especially in retrospect, some of Yanukovych's strengths—support from the oligarchs and the disillusioned and apathetic public—proved also to be weak spots when the regime came under pressure. However, despite the presence of these fissures in the nation's political landscape, predicting when the regime would come under pressure and what would trigger a full-fledged crisis was just as challenging a task as predicting the Arab Spring or many other popular uprisings. It was obvious to anyone looking at these and similar situations that the status quo was not tenable indefinitely. But who could predict when and how the breaking point would come?

It's the Economy, Stupid!

For all the political fissures he faced, Yanukovych's biggest problem was economic rather than political. The list of Ukraine's economic afflictions is as familiar as it is long—inadequate reforms, corruption, dependence on energy imported from Russia and the Russian market for exports, excessive social spending. While the country experienced a period of strong growth in the 2000's, the 2008–2009 economic crisis delivered a massive blow to its economy, with GDP falling by 15 percent.[22] The Yanukovych government had negotiated a $15 billion loan with the IMF in 2010 but was unable to fulfill the conditions attached to it, and the loan was suspended in 2011.

The critical vulnerability of the country's economy was its dependence on Russian gas. The opaque gas-trading arrangement—widely seen as corrupt—coupled with heavy gas subsidies for domestic consumers left Ukraine perennially indebted to Russia for gas deliveries.[23] The 2010 gas deal with Russia resulted in a 30 percent cut in the price of Russian gas in exchange for extended Russian access to naval facilities in Crimea, but the deal provided only temporary relief.[24] By the end of 2013, Ukraine's gas debt to Russia was estimated at $1 billion, though other estimates were considerably higher.[25,26]

Besides gas debts to Russia, the Yanukovych government was beset by several other major economic challenges, including a politically motivated commitment to an unrealistic currency peg and growing inability to borrow to sustain excessive government spending on social programs.[27,28] With the government facing over $15 billion in maturing debt in 2014, and the Central Bank reserves around $20 billion, Yanukovych attempted to get another $15 billion loan from the IMF, but it proved impossible without accepting a strict set of conditions that the Ukrainian president, facing reelection in 2015, did not want to take on, for fear of popular backlash.[29] The EU was offering a relatively small—€610 million—financial aid package for signing the AA, but it was only a fraction of what Ukraine needed to avoid defaulting on its obligations.[30] Besides, the EU insisted on Ukraine resuming its program with the IMF. With Ukrainian bond yields in excess of 10 percent, the country's prospects in capital markets looked dim.[31] But default, in a pre-election year, was not an option. Yanukovych would have to look for other sources of financing to avoid default and to save his reelection prospects in 2015.

The External Setting

Viktor Yanukovych's foreign policy record leading up to the crisis in many ways parallels his domestic performance. He wound up antagonizing all of his negotiating partners, who came to view their dealings with him and his government as an unpleasant necessity rather than as a welcome opportunity.

Discredited in the West

Burdened by the legacy of his governorship in Donetsk, rumors of his criminal past, and the compromised election of 2004 that triggered the Orange revolution, Yanukovych's reputation in the West was somewhat restored by his victory in the 2010 election, recognized as free and fair by international observers. Legitimized by the outcome of the election and promising long-delayed and much-needed series of reforms, Yanukovych had initially gained a measure of respectability and was given considerable benefit of the doubt at the outset of his presidency and even well into it.[32,33]

However, Yanukovych's actions eventually dispelled those doubts, and his reputation abroad suffered accordingly. The widespread allegations of corruption, the lack of progress on economic reforms, the failure to sustain the program with the IMF, and—perhaps most shocking to Europe and the United States—the imprisonment of Tymoshenko: all shattered the image of Yanukovych as a transformed leader.[34]

No Friend of Putin's

Curiously, Yanukovych not only succeeded in ruining his reputation in, and relations with, the West, but also managed to develop a rather difficult relationship with Russia and Putin personally. Early in his tenure, in exchange for a discount on Russian gas, he concluded an agreement to extend the Russian Black Sea fleet lease on the Sevastopol' base for an additional twenty-five years beyond its original expiration date of 2017.[35] Yanukovych also dropped the goal of eventually joining NATO from Ukrainian national security concept. Despite these concessions to Russia, Putin reportedly had a dim view of his Ukrainian counterpart.[36] Putin was also reported to have good relations with Tymoshenko and was said to favor her over Yanukovych in the 2010 election.[37] Some have attributed this tension to Yanukovych's resentment of Putin's treatment of him as a junior partner, rather than as an equal.

The personal relationship between the two presidents notwithstanding, the relationship between the two countries was strained. At issue were continuous disagreements about energy, trade, transit, and handling of past debts, and the very nature of the relationship between them. Moscow wanted a closer association, envisioning Ukrainian membership first in the Eurasian Customs Union (CU) and later in the Eurasian Economic Union. Kyiv resisted both—undoubtedly a major irritant to Russian policymakers, as well as to Putin personally, who embraced the cause of Eurasian integration as one of his flagship initiatives in his third presidential term and as an economic and geopolitical counterweight to the EU.[38]

Despite his unwillingness to join the CU, Yanukovych engaged in protracted negotiations with Putin to establish some other relationship with Russia, one that would fall short of full CU membership. An outright refusal on Yanukovych's part to join the CU undoubtedly would have led to more Russian economic and political pressure on

Ukraine—particularly in the area of energy trade, but also in bilateral trade in general, which was of great importance to a large segment of the country's economy dependent on the Russian market, which accounts for some 25 percent of Ukrainian exports.[39]

While negotiating with Putin, Yanukovych also was engaged in protracted and complicated talks with the EU about signing the AA and DCFTA. These negotiations began in 2007 and 2008 respectively, and in 2012 the two sides initialed the texts of both documents.[40] However, the final stage of the negotiations proceeded slowly, suggesting that Yanukovych was reluctant to accept the demanding conditions of the two documents, which called for wide-ranging legislative and regulatory changes that he almost certainly was unwilling to undertake for fear of undercutting his own power and authority. In retrospect, it appears that Yanukovych was more interested in the negotiations themselves than in their outcome: because EU negotiators viewed the AA and DCFTA as incompatible with membership in the CU, the negotiations provided Yanukovych a hedge against Russian pressure.[41]

Putin and Yanukovych had conducted many meetings since Putin's reelection for his third presidential term, including some allegedly secret meetings; they failed, however, to arrive at a mutually acceptable deal.[42] The Russian president's contempt for his Ukrainian counterpart as a weak and indecisive leader was confirmed after Yanukovych's unexpected flight for asylum in Russia.[43] Contempt was perhaps the only thing that the Russian president shared with his European and U.S. counterparts with respect to Ukraine.

The United States is Busy

During the years before the crisis in late 2013, Ukraine had occupied a relatively low place on the foreign policy agenda of the United States. This low priority was the consequence of both temporal and structural factors. The temporal factor had to do with the sheer number of other major foreign policy and national security challenges on the U.S. agenda, including the 2008 war in Georgia and its aftermath, the Arab Spring, the civil war in Syria, the wars in Iraq and Afghanistan, and nuclear talks with Iran, as well as the "reset" with Russia.

The structural factor had to do with the relatively limited toolbox available to the United States for engaging with Ukraine. Yanukovych's domestic agenda, focused on unbridled accumulation of political power and wealth, left few opportunities for U.S. promotion of reform in Ukraine. The desire to isolate the Yanukovych regime following Tymoshenko's trial and imprisonment was also undoubtedly a factor. The structural limitation on U.S. ability to sustain engagement with Ukraine was also a byproduct of Washington's having traditionally taken the lead (with Europe following) in preparing Eastern Europe's new democracies for membership in NATO.[44] This course of action was not available to Washington either.

President Viktor Yushchenko's government had expressed interest in joining NATO and asked the alliance to prepare a Membership Action Plan (MAP).[45] Ukraine had participated in several international operations with the United States—with NATO in the Balkans, and with the international coalition in Iraq. At the 2008 NATO summit in Bucharest, the allies declared that they welcomed Ukraine's, along with Georgia's, Euro-Atlantic aspirations and that "these nations will become members of NATO."[46]

However, upon his election to the presidency, Yanukovych took a different path and distanced himself from his predecessor's pursuit of NATO membership.[47] Yanukovych chose instead a non-aligned status for Ukraine. That stance corresponded to the mood of the Ukrainian public, which had long been divided on the issue of NATO membership. According to a Gallup poll, in 2008, 43 percent of Ukrainians saw NATO as a threat, 15 percent saw it as a source of protection, and 30 percent were indifferent.[48] In 2013, 17 percent saw it as a threat, 29 percent saw it as a source of protection, and 44 percent were indifferent.

The law on non-alignment passed in the Ukrainian parliament in 2010, but it left ample room for Ukraine to continue to participate in NATO's Partnership for Peace (PfP) exercises and other activities. These arrangements entailed regular visits by senior NATO defense and military figures, Ukrainian participation in NATO training activities, and even NATO military exercises on Ukrainian territory. This activity had become routine, even though it triggered local protests in some areas where it was conducted, most notably in Crimea.[49]

Given Yanukovych's withdrawal from the path of NATO membership, U.S. engagement options with Ukraine were limited at best. Most important for U.S. policy, however, was the somewhat abstract nature of U.S. interests in Ukraine. Ukraine's decision to surrender its portion of the Soviet nuclear arsenal deployed on its territory and accede to the Non-Proliferation Treaty (NPT) as a non-nuclear state had removed the single most important concern from the U.S. agenda in Ukraine. And compared to European interests, U.S. interests in Ukraine were quite intangible. The United States had made a general commitment to help former Soviet states make a successful transition to capitalism and democracy and to integrate in the international community; it was committed to seeing Ukraine succeed in its transformation into a stable democracy, but only as a matter of general U.S. democracy-building the world over. It also had an interest, of course, in preventing the re-emergence of Russia as an imperial state, both as an extension of U.S. commitment to the security of Europe and as a consequence of the popular argument that an imperial Russia could not become a democracy and a true partner to the United States.[50]

By contrast, Europe had a direct, tangible stake in Ukraine, first and foremost as a key transit state for Russian gas. A close neighbor whose stability and security are closely tied to the rest of the continent, especially to the easternmost EU member-states, Ukraine was a key concern for the EU. The burden of formulating the policy of the transatlantic community's policy toward Ukraine—and the subsequent burden of leading the community in its implementation—thus fell to Europe. As if to complement this, then Prime Minister Mykola Azarov stated, when he submitted the non-alignment legislation to the parliament, that Ukraine's priority would be European integration.[51]

Europe Gets to Lead

Europe was also limited in the amount of attention it could give to Ukraine. As with the United States, this was the result of both temporal and structural factors. The EU was preoccupied with its own internal crises—in Greece, Italy, Spain—as well as with the very future of the union, threatened by disagreement among its key members about the scale and scope of integration and the role of its key political and economic institutions. In this context, Ukraine appeared neither as a serious problem needing immediate attention nor as an opportunity to be seized.

Structurally, the EU's policy toward its eastern neighbors was defined by the Eastern Partnership (EP), a subset of the EU's general European Neighborhood Policy (ENP) developed in 2004. The EP focused specifically on the EU's eastern neighbors in the former USSR, states that were not serious candidates for membership in the Union. But the ENP appeared more like a transformation and reform policy than a foreign policy. According to the official description of the ENP, its objective is

> avoiding the emergence of new dividing lines between the enlarged EU and our neighbours and instead strengthening the prosperity, stability and security of all. It is based on the values of democracy, rule of law and respect of human rights.[52]

In any event, a common European foreign policy toward Ukraine would have been unrealistic given the diversity of European interests in Ukraine—which ranged from quite remote, in the case of Portugal, to vital, in the case of Poland. The emphasis on shared values of democracy, rule of law and respect for human rights made the application of this policy to Yanukovych's Ukraine a highly ambitious transformational enterprise.

For all the institutional reforms called for in the ENP and EP—emphasizing compatibility with EU laws, regulations, and practices—they did not include an explicit reference to prospects for joining the EU. Rather, the question of EU membership was left ambiguously open. Such a possibility was not ruled out, but it was not on offer either. A successful reform program was obviously a necessary condition for eventually joining the EU, but it was not sufficient. Europe's eastern

borders would be secured by making its neighbors more like—
but not necessarily members of—the EU.

Though the ENP did not explicitly aim to create a wider
sphere of EU influence or a collection of satellites subservient
to Western Europe, the ENP's practical effect would still have
amounted to creating a peripheral region where it would exert
considerable influence. Extensive trade and economic relations
would involve the EU as the dominant partner, and the EU
would enjoy expanded political and cultural influence through
extension of its economic might. The Association Agreements
(AA) negotiated by the EU with ENP countries carried extensive and ambitious free trade protocols under the title of a Deep
and Comprehensive Free Trade Area (DCFTA), which committed ENP countries to adopt and implement EU laws in areas of
trade, consumer protection, and environmental regulation.[53] In
a word, Brussels's writ would be extended well beyond the European Union's borders to countries that were not even on the
path toward EU membership.

The ENP and the EP emerged, then, as substitutes for a common EU foreign policy, as well as for its expansion policy. The
goals of making the Eastern neighbors more EU-like and binding
them closer to the EU economically, but without offering them
a path to membership or setting any other explicit or implicit
requirements, was effectively the lowest common denominator
that would suit both the newest members of the EU concerned
about securing their periphery and older members worried about
the costs of expansion.

Although based on the premise of expanding European values and norms, and thus an idealistic enterprise, the ENP and the
EP undoubtedly had a geopolitical dimension as well. Among
their most active proponents were the EU's newest members,

all of which were former Soviet satellites: worried about being Europe's new edge and the prospect of instability on their periphery, they were eager to secure their borders by stabilizing and binding their eastern neighbors closer to Europe by a common European framework.[54] The fact that all of Europe's eastern neighbors were vulnerable to Russian pressure only added to these anxieties. Poland and Sweden—both countries with histories of difficult relations with Russia—emerged as initiators and leading advocates of the EP.[55,56,57]

Ukraine was both the biggest and the most important country participating in the EP. By binding Ukraine to Europe and pulling it away from Russia, Poland and its EU partners could gain a huge margin of safety in the form of an additional buffer zone between Poland-Slovakia-Hungary-Romania and Russia. The EU would gain additional leverage over Russia by denying it control of the Ukrainian gas transport system that carried vast quantities of Russian gas to Europe and weaken Russia's leverage over Europe. The confluence of idealistic goals and geopolitical interests was obvious.

Talks between Ukraine and the EU on the terms of the AA began in March 2007, while talks on the DCFTA followed in February 2008. Negotiating such deals is an ambitious and lengthy undertaking with many stakeholders on both sides. Ukraine, with its chaotic transitional political system and insecure democratic governance, its widespread corruption, powerful oligarchs, and largely unreformed economy, presented a particularly difficult case for EU negotiators seeking to commit the country to the path of democracy, free market, and rule of law.

Negotiations suffered a further setback following the trial and imprisonment of Tymoshenko. Her fate and reputation as a strong advocate of European integration for Ukraine under-scored the shortcomings of the Yanukovych presidency and the difficulty of negotiating with a leader who had deliberately chosen to curtail the country's democratic freedoms, pervert its justice, and engage in massive corruption and electoral fraud. Tymoshenko's release from prison became one of the key demands imposed by EU negotiators as a precondition for the signing of the AA and DCFTA with Ukraine.[58] With no sign of Yanukovych's intent to pardon her and the fate of the AA at stake, the jailed opposition leader appealed to EU leaders to sign the AA with Ukraine anyway as a strategic move designed to bring Ukraine closer to Europe.[59]

Despite numerous EU missions and intense diplomatic pressure, the Ukrainian president would not budge.[60] Presented with the choice of following the high principle and scuttling the AA and the DCFTA at the November 2013 Vilnius summit, the EU was poised to put principle aside, follow its interest, and sign the documents with Ukraine's compromised leader.

Russia's Position

Russia's policy toward Ukraine in the lead-up to the crisis was framed by two connected themes of Russian foreign policy. The first was the long-standing Russian resentment of the West's geopolitical expansion into areas of traditional Russian interest and domination. The expansion of NATO, and subsequently of the EU, has long been seen by the Russian foreign policy establishment as an attempt by the United States and its European allies to marginalize Russia, diminish its role in European and global affairs, and weaken its security and economic and political influence.

Russian opposition to NATO enlargement is well known. Almost immediately upon the start of discussions in Washington, Brussels, and elsewhere in Europe about expanding the alliance eastward, it became clear that despite claims about the end of the Cold War and willingness to cooperate with the alliance, Russia remained deeply suspicious of its purpose, maintaining that the alliance had no purpose after the end of the Cold War and should follow the example of the Warsaw pact and dissolve itself. Though explained by NATO's leaders as a step *toward* Russia—intended to bring the zone of stability, security and prosperity closer to Russia's borders—the expansion of the alliance has always been viewed by Moscow as Western expansion *against* Russia and a betrayal of the spirit, if not the letter, of the terms on which the United States and the Soviet Union had agreed to end the Cold War.[61]

Putin delivered one of the most authoritative denunciations of NATO's expansion at the Munich Security Conference in 2007. Speaking to an audience of senior officials and prominent security experts from both sides of the Atlantic, he charged that

> NATO expansion does not have any relation with the modernization of the Alliance itself or with ensuring security in Europe. On the contrary, it represents a serious provocation that reduces the level of mutual trust. And we have the right to ask: against whom is this expansion intended? And what happened to the assurances our western partners made after the dissolution of the Warsaw Pact? Where are those declarations today? No one even remembers them. But I will allow myself to remind this audience what was said. I would like to quote the speech of NATO General Secretary Mr. Woerner in Brussels on 17 May 1990. He said at the time that "the fact that we are ready not to place a NATO army outside of German territory gives the Soviet Union a firm security guarantee." Where are these guarantees?[62]

For many in Russia's national security establishment, NATO enlargement was possible only because of Russia's weakness during the 1990s. Its political stabilization and economic recovery in the new century made it possible for it to "rise from its knees," rebuild a measure of its lost military muscle, stand up to Western pressure, and prevent further expansion of the alliance to the territories of the former Soviet Union—including to Ukraine and Georgia, both of which were marked for NATO membership at the 2008 summit in Bucharest.[63]

The second theme, also long-standing, but endowed with new urgency during the third presidential term of Vladimir Putin, was Eurasian integration: the gathering of former Soviet states in an economic, political, and security ring centered around Russia. Eurasian integration was intended to provide Russia with an added measure of security against perceived Western encroachment and enhance Russia's standing as a major power. As a leading Russian foreign policy expert has put it, no major power "walks alone."[64]

Perhaps the clearest formulation of Russian attitudes toward the West belongs to then-president Dmitri Medvedev, who in the aftermath of the 2008 war with Georgia declared the neighboring states a zone of Russia's "privileged interests."[65] The implicit but transparent message to other powers, and in particular to the Unites States, was unambiguous: "respect the primacy of Russia in these lands and best of all keep out." The war with Georgia, clearly intended to punish the small neighbor for its Western geopolitical orientation and desire to escape Russia's sphere of influence, sent a powerful signal to other former Soviet states not to push the boundaries of Moscow's patience. It also sent a message to the West to tread lightly in Russia's neighborhood.

Focused on hard power and military threats, Russian leaders concentrated their energies and rhetoric on NATO as the principal challenge to Russia. The EU elicited significantly less attention and ire from Russian policymakers than did NATO, if only because it played a much smaller and less visible role in the immediate periphery of Russia, choosing instead to focus efforts and resources on countries of Central Europe with immediate prospects of membership.

The absence of a collective military dimension in the EU underscored the difference between the two organizations and contributed to Russian preoccupation with NATO. Moreover, whereas the EU did not entertain plans for expansion into the former Soviet Union beyond the Baltic states, and its engagement with the former Soviet states did not entail a path toward membership, NATO did make explicit membership commitments to Georgia and Ukraine and worked with them to devise a path to membership.

Besides NATO enlargement—or perhaps as a direct complement to it—Moscow had grown resentful of U.S. democracy promotion in former Soviet states. Moscow saw Western efforts in this area as yet another form of geopolitical encirclement of Russia and even as a deliberate policy of spreading of instability *inside* Russia. Western support for the so-called "color revolutions" in Georgia in 2003, in Ukraine in 2004, and in Kyrgyzstan in 2005 were seen in a similar light. Western endorsement of large-scale anti-Putin protests in the winter of 2011–2012—along with visible disapproval of the fact and the manner of the Russian leader's return to the presidency in an election viewed in the West as deeply compromised—was interpreted by Putin as evidence of Western plans to destabilize Russia through democracy promotion. Putin expressed Russian resentment of these policies most recently in a July 2014 speech to senior Foreign Ministry personnel and described them as a form of Cold War–style containment of Russia by the West: "The events in Ukraine are the concentrated expression of the policy of containing Russia. The roots of this policy go deep into history, it is clear that this policy, unfortunately, did not end with the Cold War."[66]

However, despite continuing Russian preoccupation with NATO, the EU began to figure more prominently as a challenge to Russian policy of rebuilding a sphere of influence in the former Soviet space. This was due to both the EU's growing attention to its eastern neighborhood and Ukraine in particular, and to Russia's reinvigorated policy of Eurasian integration as a major foreign policy objective in Putin's third term.[67] The plan was to stitch together as many of the former Soviet states as possible into a Russian-dominated Customs Union. It is to be followed by closer political integration with a Russian-dominated supranational decision-making body under the name of Eurasian Union.[68]

Ukraine—the second most populous former Soviet state with the second largest economy after Russia—was by far the most important target of Putin's integration policy. With Russian emphasis on hard power and territorial control, Europe's pursuit of an AA with Ukraine, across whose territory Russia sends 15 percent of Europe's gas supply, no doubt looked like yet another threatening geopolitical step in a series intended to undercut Russian leverage.[69] Aside from its size, its location between Russia and Europe and its infrastructure—so important to Russia's gas trade with Europe—made Ukraine absolutely critical to Putin's plans for Eurasian integration and to Russia's sense of security. For Putin, as a statesman and Russian leader, the "loss" of Ukraine to the EU for the second time, after he had "lost" Ukraine during the 2004 Orange Revolution, was not an outcome he was prepared to accept.

The Competition Heats Up

With two competing blueprints for the future of Ukraine—one from the EU and one from Russia—an outright competition was only a matter of time. By 2013, discussions between Kyiv and Moscow about the former's membership in the Russian-led CU had been going on for several years, at least since the CU's inception in 2010.[70] The main attraction for Ukraine in joining the CU was the promise from Russia that Ukraine would be able to buy Russian gas at a much lower price.[71]

The formal obstacles to Ukraine's membership in the CU were threefold: the clause in the Ukrainian constitution prohibiting delegation of decision-making authorities to supranational bodies, Ukraine's obligations to the WTO, and the incompatibility between CU and AA/DCFTA terms.[72] The informal and more decisive obstacle was Yanukovych's desire to extract maximum benefits from Europe and Russia while keeping both at arm's length and retaining flexibility to maneuver between them to suit his political preferences.[73]

Ukraine's progress in AA and DCFTA negotiations appears to have driven the Russian response. With talks between Ukraine and the EU entering the final stage, Moscow pushed for progress in its own talks with Kyiv about joining the CU. In June 2013, Ukraine agreed to become an observer at the CU—a step closer, but well short of membership.[74] Almost immediately, Sergey Glaz'yev, Putin's adviser and a key advocate of Eurasian integration, publicly threatened Ukraine that it would lose its observer status in the CU should it sign a DCFTA.[75]

Russian pressure continued to mount. In July 2013, Russia imposed a ban on several categories of Ukrainian imports—confectionery and dairy products (because of alleged health concerns) as well as pipe. In addition, Russian customs officials introduced lengthy inspections at the border with Ukraine, halting traffic and imperiling the flow of Ukrainian goods—many of them perishable—to Russia.[76] The economic toll from these punitive actions was estimated to lie between $500 million and $2.5 billion, and the threat of more sanctions from Russia posed a major threat to Ukraine's fragile economy.[77] However, despite the propaganda campaign and the trade sanctions, Ukraine appeared on course to sign the AA and DCFTA at the November 28–29 EU summit in Vilnius.

The November Surprise

The surprise came a week before the Vilnius summit. On November 21, Yanukovych abruptly ordered that the AA and DCFTA talks be suspended. With little explanation, both agreements were frozen, and the government of Ukraine announced that it was resuming talks with Russia about CU membership.[78]

Yanukovich's about-face came after unprecedented pressure from Russia and secret talks with Putin at an airport near Moscow on November 9.[79] Following that, Yanukovych's prime minister, Mykola Azarov, met with his Russian counterpart, Dmitri Medvedev, for further talks that the former described as "most productive."[80]

Within a month, on December 17, Russia announced a massive aid package consisting of $15 billion in loans on terms highly favorable to Ukraine and deep—roughly 30 percent—gas discounts amounting to between $3.5 and $7 billion in 2014.[81]

What Yanukovych had promised to do for Putin in exchange for such largesse was not clear. But he received the lifeline he so desperately needed to avoid default in 2014 without spending cuts, especially gas subsidy cuts, in a pre-election year.

The generous size of the aid package suggests that Putin had a strong interest in settling the issue of Russian-Ukrainian relations—if not once and for all, then at least for a considerable period of time. He certainly had a powerful incentive to do so, since the Sochi Winter Olympic Games were scheduled to start in February. Sochi had become a matter of personal prestige for Putin, who wanted to demonstrate to the world and to Russia the country's progress under his leadership. With numerous foreign heads of state and other dignitaries invited, he did not want the unrest in Ukraine and the tug of war over it with the West to serve as the backdrop for the games.

However, in the month between Yanukovych's abrupt withdrawal from AA and DCFTA negotiations and the announcement of the massive Russian aid package, Ukrainian domestic politics underwent a radical transformation. EU officials were stunned by Yanukovych's about-face, so near the end of a protracted negotiation. What is more, it shocked the people of Ukraine out of their political apathy and brought them out into the streets by the tens and eventually even hundreds of thousands. The situation was beyond Yanukovych's ability to control it—and Putin's ability to influence it with cash.

As late as September 2013, the Ukrainian public appeared ambivalent on the issue of closer association with the EU: 42 percent favored joining the EU while 37 percent favored CU membership.[82] Yet the response to Yanukovych's backtracking from the signing in Vilnius was quick and unequivocal.

On November 24—the first Sunday after Yanukovych's stunning announcement—an estimated 100,000 protesters went out into the streets in Kyiv in what was described as the largest public anti-government protests since the 2004 Orange Revolution. Protesters called for Yanukovych to rescind his decree freezing talks with the EU and for his and his government's resignation. Some threw stones and firebombs at police, who responded with tear gas to break up the demonstrations.[83] With protests continuing and police ramping up violence to crack down on protesters, most of them peaceful, Yanukovych became the target of not only domestic opposition, but also growing international condemnation.[84]

With neither side in the standoff willing to yield, violence escalated in the center of Kyiv. Early December protests drew an estimated 800,000 people. Protesters seized Kyiv's city hall and set up a fortified tent city in Independence Square, triggering more violent action by police.[85] On December 10, police violently attempted to storm the encampment in Independence Square, which resulted in more casualties and arrests of some of the protesters. U.S. Secretary of State John Kerry issued a statement expressing "disgust with the decision of Ukrainian authorities to meet the peaceful protest in Kyiv's Maidan Square with riot police, bulldozers, and batons, rather than with respect for democratic rights and human dignity."[86]

Despite domestic and international condemnation of Yanukovych's actions and violence against protesters, the standoff continued. Yanukovych's success in obtaining a major aid package from Russia failed to convince the protesters of the benefit of closer association with Russia. Protests spread beyond Kyiv to western Ukraine, and even to some cities in eastern Ukraine.

The new normal in Ukrainian politics was broken in mid-January by the parliament when it passed a set of laws intended to make protests illegal and severely constrain the ability of the opposition to resist the government. But the new legislation only breathed new energy into the opposition and led to more protests, which triggered a new violent crackdown by the authorities that resulted in new casualties, including several fatalities. By the end of January the laws were repealed, and the cabinet of Prime Minister Mykola Azarov resigned.[87]

Throughout the crisis, Yanukovych and the opposition engaged in talks about a compromise solution. In mid-February, the parties agreed that the opposition would vacate some of the buildings it had occupied throughout the protests, and the government released the protesters arrested since the beginning of the protests in December.[88]

However, despite these signs of progress, on February 18 more violence erupted in central Kyiv. What incited it has remained unclear, but it left 18 dead on both sides, as well as hundreds wounded. On February 20, more violence followed with the number of casualties increasing rapidly—88 new deaths were reported, many of them from sniper fire against protesters.[89]

The new round of violence appears to have shocked the government into agreeing to a truce. On February 21, the opposition and the government signed a compromise agreement whose key points included restoration of the 2004 constitution that enhanced the powers of the prime minister at the expense of those of the president, formation of a new government of national unity, further constitutional reform to be completed in September 2014, and a new presidential election in December 2014.[90] However, upon signing the agreement, which was endorsed by EU representatives with apparent Russian concurrence, Yanukovych fled the capital and effectively abandoned the presidency. On February 25, the parliament voted formally to remove him from office and set the new election date for May 25.[91]

Yanukovych's flight has never been fully explained. The most likely explanation appears to be his lack of confidence in his own security apparatus, fear of imprisonment, or even violent death at the hands of protesters, who, he probably thought, would not accept the terms of the deal negotiated by opposition leaders and would proceed to overthrow his government and hunt him down.[92]

The Yanukovych chapter of Ukrainian history had ended. A new chapter began.

Russia Moves on Crimea

The sudden disintegration of the Yanukovych regime was a stunning surprise to Western policymakers. It must have come as a shock to the Kremlin as well. While blaming the West for supporting unrest in Ukraine as an attempted coup, the Kremlin also spared no criticism of Yanukovych as an incompetent leader unable to deal with the crisis effectively, and, if needed, by force.[93] Putin's own dismissive comments about Yanukovych soon after he fled to Russia were probably indicative of the poor relationship between the two leaders, reinforced by his handling of the crisis.[94] The speed and scale of political change in Ukraine must have been breathtaking for Russian leaders, suddenly left without an obvious partner in Kyiv and, most likely, without a clear plan of action.

Russian decision-making during the pivotal phase of the crisis in Ukraine was no doubt affected by the fact that Russian leadership, and especially Putin—who by all accounts had personally taken charge of Ukraine policy—was preoccupied with the Sochi Winter Olympics.[95] The tensions surrounding the games conducted near Russia's turbulent North Caucasus provinces and Georgia—along with the widespread reporting of corruption, shoddy workmanship, and poor security at the games—had ensured that Russian leaders would be focused on Sochi. The closing ceremony on February 23 proved to be a resounding success: the games went smoothly, and Russia emerged as the country receiving the most medals.

Planned as a triumph of Russian recovery and renewed international standing, the games were indeed a success. However, the fall of Yanukovych and the victory of the pro-Western and anti-Russian opposition in Kyiv cast a dark shadow on that success and presented the Kremlin with few options to repair the damage. The reputations of Russia and Putin were at stake, especially considering Putin's earlier apparent success with Ukraine. The February reversal was dramatic and put Putin at risk of a historic defeat.

The perception of a historic loss was compounded by the presence in Kyiv, throughout the crucial days of the crisis, of senior European officials who did little to conceal their support for the opposition and their disapproval of the Yanukovych presidency and its ties to Russia. This show of disapproval undoubtedly fed Russian suspicions that the fall of Yanukovych was part of a carefully planned Western action. Moreover, a well-publicized intercept of a telephone conversation between two senior U.S. officials overseeing U.S. policy in Ukraine, in which they discussed the likely composition of the post-Yanukovych government, undoubtedly inflamed Russian suspicions of a Western, U.S.-led plot to turn Ukraine into a U.S.-EU satellite state.[96]

With the Kremlin's game plan overturned by developments in Kyiv well beyond its control, and with few alternatives, it had to act quickly and decisively to prevent Ukraine from slipping away. What options were open to it? With the revolutionary fervor sweeping Kyiv—much, if not most, of it anti-Russian and all of it fueled by the Ukrainian public's desire for closer ties to Europe and fewer ties to Russia—political dialogue did not look promising. Economic tools—the $15 billion loan and gas discounts of up to $7 billion—had not done the job. An outright military invasion no doubt looked daunting.

The Kremlin did have one tool that had proved its utility as an instrument of Russian policy in its neighborhood—local separatism. It had been used and worked well in Transnistria, Abkhazia, and South Ossetia by creating permanent frozen conflicts that became Russian outposts for protecting and projecting Russian power and influence. Crimea, with a major Russian military base, majority Russian population, many retirees from the Soviet Armed Forces and the Russian Navy, and a history of difficult relations and separatist aspirations in the 1990s, was a prime target for inflicting a wound that would undermine Ukraine's sovereignty and territorial integrity and create a pressure point to influence Ukraine's behavior.

Given the long history of Russian-Ukrainian tensions over Crimea, the Russian military almost certainly had prepared and refined blueprints for an operation there to seize control of the peninsula. It did not take long for the first signs of the operation to manifest themselves. Pro-Russian demonstrations began in Crimea on February 23, and by March 1 Crimea was no longer under the control of the government of Ukraine.[97]

Was the annexation of Crimea by Russia, which followed shortly thereafter, part of a carefully constructed plan? Unlikely.

Given the speed with which events in Crimea and in Kyiv progressed, the Kremlin probably found itself in a reactive mode. The outpouring of support for its action by both the residents of Crimea and the Russian citizenry probably motivated the Kremlin to act boldly and proceed with the referendum and the annexation. Russian public opinion supportive of the annexation was fueled by a fierce propaganda campaign in the Russian media, which—with few exceptions—portrayed the revolution in Ukraine as a Western plot executed by radical Ukrainian nationalists and fascist elements. With the public firmly behind it, the Kremlin had no reason to hesitate.

However, the seizure of Crimea raised a number of new challenges for the Kremlin. Chief among them was what to do next. The annexation of Crimea had only deepened the divide between Kyiv and Moscow and stiffened the resolve of the new government of Ukraine to proceed with its plans for closer integration with Europe. Whereas in September of 2013 50 percent of Ukrainian citizens had a "warm" attitude toward Russia, in April 2014, 73 percent opposed Russia sending its troops to Ukraine to protect Russian-speakers.[98,99] Instead of ensuring Russian influence in Ukraine, the annexation of Crimea had severely eroded it.

In charting the new course, the Kremlin had to contend with a wave of international condemnation, sanctions, and threats of more sanctions to come. The relationship with Ukraine had been badly damaged and seemed destined to remain so for the foreseeable future. At the same time, domestic support for the Kremlin's policy was at an all time high.[100] Taken together, these circumstances presented a powerful argument against reconciliation, which carried the risk of appearing weak both abroad and at home. With Russia traditionally disinclined to soft power, accommodation was unlikely.

The alternative was maintaining pressure on Ukraine and—if circumstances warranted—escalation. This logic, combined with Russia's previous experience of assuring its regional influence with the help of frozen conflicts and applying both hard power and the threat of using it, emerged as the key driver of Russian policy toward Ukraine in the spring and summer of 2014. It was probably reinforced by the perception that Ukraine's elite and public were overwhelmingly in favor of European integration and that without sustained Russian pressure Ukraine would be lost to Europe.

The Kremlin's actions in the months following the annexation of Crimea—massing troops on the Ukrainian border, threatening military intervention, recruiting and dispatching combatants and weaponry to eastern Ukraine, occupying government buildings there, launching the concept of Novorossiya that would include eastern and southern Ukraine as a vast separatist enclave, establishing self-proclaimed republics in Luhansk and Donetsk, campaigning to disrupt the May 25 presidential election—seem to have been designed to undermine Ukraine's territorial integrity and sovereignty, and to demonstrate the incompetence and the illegitimate nature of the new Ukrainian government, as well as the danger associated with the course of European integration it was following.

Russia has had to scale back its apparent ambitions for establishing a vast protectorate under the name of Novorossiya in southern and eastern Ukraine.[101] That vision apparently exceeded the resources the Kremlin was prepared to commit, as well as the support of the local population.

At the same time, Russia has also demonstrated its commitment to maintain separatist enclaves in the Luhansk and Donetsk regions and to prevent Ukraine from accomplishing a victory on the battlefield and wiping out the separatist insurgency. With the separatists on the verge of being defeated by pro-Kyiv forces in late summer of 2014, the Kremlin stepped up its involvement in the conflict and sent in military personnel, weapons, and supplies. The gains of the pro-Kyiv forces were reversed; they suffered heavy losses, and the Ukrainian government was forced to sign a ceasefire agreement in September that called for significant concessions to the separatists and Russia.[102]

Eastern Ukraine: A Stalemate

Eastern Ukraine is settling into a stalemate. Though the ceasefire has been violated frequently and could well collapse, it was the best choice among a set of unattractive options. For Moscow, the Luhansk-Donetsk region represents an opportunity to establish a protectorate inside Ukraine and thus gain a springboard for projecting Russian influence into Ukraine. Crimea can no longer serve that purpose now that it has been annexed by Russia. For Kyiv, the ceasefire offers a respite from the fighting that was draining resources it could ill afford to spend on a conflict it could not win against insurgents backed by a superior adversary. Eastern Ukraine therefore appears set to become another frozen conflict.

3 Impact of the Crisis on Russia

In his 1997 book *The Grand Chessboard*, Zbigniew Brzezinski stressed the importance of Ukraine as the key to Russia's future.[1] With Ukraine, he argued, Russia is destined to remain an empire; without it, it is not. The crisis in Ukraine has left a deep and, by all indicators, lasting impact on Russia—both its domestic politics and its foreign policy.

Neither the domestic change in Russia nor the change in its foreign policy represents a radical departure from the course followed by the Kremlin for several years. But they do represent an unprecedented hardening of the Kremlin's positions. The crisis will almost certainly come to be viewed as a major turning point in Russian domestic development and its foreign policy.

Domestic Political Entrenchment

Domestically, the crisis in Ukraine has resulted in a consolidation of Russian public opinion around the Kremlin's messages of Russian resurgence as a great power, vigorous patriotism, and expansionist visions of Slavic solidarity—all themes actively promoted by the majority of the Russian media. In July 2014, Putin's approval rating reached 85 percent—even after the shootdown of the Malaysian airliner over Ukraine and the universal international condemnation of Russian actions in Ukraine that followed it. Sixty-four percent thought that unrest in eastern Ukraine was the result of interference by the West.[2] Fifty-five percent favored active Russian support for the separatists in eastern Ukraine.[3] Sixty-one percent were not concerned about the West's economic sanctions imposed on Russia, and 58 percent were not worried about their country's international isolation.[4]

The patriotic surge that has accompanied the annexation of Crimea and the confrontation with the West is neither a surprising nor a new phenomenon in Russian domestic politics. The key message broadcast by major Russian media outlets, especially the state-controlled TV channels, is that Putin's Russia has entered a stage of ideological, political, and geopolitical competition with the West. Although Russian state-controlled TV and other media have long broadcast significant amounts of anti-American and anti-Western propaganda, the intensity of such propaganda increased after Putin's reelection to his third presidential term in 2012, an election that was accompanied by major protests in Russia and was criticized in the West as flawed.[5] Putin accused the United States—in particular, Secretary of State Hillary Clinton—of stirring protests in Russia.[6] In his election-night speech the tearful president-elect charged that his opponents were enemies of Russia, intent on destroying it.[7]

Putin's reelection was followed by a series of new legislative and administrative initiatives that sought to limit political freedoms and minimize foreign, especially Western, influence in Russian domestic politics. These have included requiring nongovernmental organizations receiving foreign aid to register as foreign agents, the expulsion of U.S. Agency for International

Development (USAID) from Russia, and prosecution of protesters. In October 2014, Putin signed off on a new law limiting foreign ownership of newspapers and other media outlets to 20 percent.[8] And in a sign of potential further efforts to insulate Russia from the West, also in October 2014, the Russian Security Council discussed measures to enhance Internet security, including possibly disconnecting Russian Internet from the rest of the world in the event of an emergency.[9]

Much of this activity was undertaken to highlight the malignant effects of Western involvement in Russian political and social life and the difference between Russia's healthy national traditions and unhealthy foreign influences. A campaign against gays and lesbians had a prominent place in this effort, as did the new legislative ban to U.S. adoptions of Russian orphans. A partnership with the Russian Orthodox Church was an important element of this effort as well.[10]

It was an easy progression, then, from the xenophobic anti-Western campaign that followed Putin's reelection to an even stronger anti-Western message that swept Russian airwaves after the annexation of Crimea and the strongly negative reaction it elicited from Western capitals. Putin's own speech upon the annexation of Crimea branded domestic critics as a "fifth column," and "national traitors" inimical to Russian national interests and hostile to Russian traditions and culture.[11] The Russian Ministry of Culture report on education and teaching of history in schools stressed the unique and distinct quality of Russia as a civilization, and proudly embraced the slogan "Russia is not Europe."[12] The crisis in Ukraine, it seems, propelled Russia to the next—more authoritarian and xenophobic—stage in its domestic political evolution.

Economic Nationalism

This political retrenchment and estrangement from the West set the stage for similar developments in the economic sphere. These economic changes were precipitated by the imposition of economic sanctions on Russia by the United States and Europe, but had been set in motion even before the onset of the Ukraine crisis.

Some steps, such as banning government officials from owning foreign bank accounts and property, were passed in 2013. Although economic in nature, the ban was widely interpreted as a move by the Kremlin to ensure tighter control of the Russian elite and minimize the potential for foreign influence or pressure on members of the establishment by foreign governments.[13] In addition, in April 2014, employees of Russian security agencies were banned from traveling to some 150 countries as an additional security step.[14]

In the defense-industrial sector, reliance on foreign suppliers has been seen for some time as a potential vulnerability the West could exploit in a crisis. Self-reliance has also been perceived as a matter of national pride. The deputy prime minister in charge of the defense industry, Dmitry Rogozin, a long-time politician known for his nationalist views and reliance on patriotic rhetoric, had emerged as the leading advocate of "buy Russian" for the Russian military.[15] The Ukraine crisis and the several rounds of sanctions imposed by the United States and the EU on Russia, including a ban on military sales, have strengthened Rogozin's argument for domestic self-sufficiency in armaments production. The sanctions, he maintained, would only strengthen the Russian defense industry, which was perfectly capable of developing and producing substitutes for imported armaments.[16]

Signaling the government's commitment to self-sufficiency in supplying the military with the best and the latest weaponry, Putin personally convened a meeting of the Commission for Military Technology Cooperation with Foreign States and assigned to it the urgent task of developing domestic substitutes for foreign weapons systems and equipment currently relied upon by the Russian military. According to reports from the meeting, Russian companies had already developed domestic substitutes for nearly one quarter of some 200 defense-related imports, with 40 more planned by 2020. The rest, Putin said, should be developed and produced domestically as soon as possible, irrespective of the cost.[17]

Economic nationalism and domestic self-sufficiency have not been limited to the defense industries. In April, in his annual report to the parliament, Prime Minister Dmitry Medvedev stated that the threat of Western sanctions was forcing Russia to reduce its reliance on foreign imports and develop domestic substitutes.[18] In May, Putin tasked the cabinet with developing broad measures to stimulate domestic manufacturing to replace foreign imports in industry in general and in agriculture in particular. In a related move to assure domestic control of Russian industry—especially large, "system-forming," or "too big to fail" enterprises of national, strategic importance—Putin directed the government to develop steps that would place offshore-owned industries under Russian jurisdiction.[19]

Some of Russia's greater vulnerabilities are likely to lie in the financial sector, where Western sanctions have already taken a toll on the economy, prompting the government to consider countermeasures. These include proposals for a national payments system to replace MasterCard and Visa, a Russian rating agency, as well as a BRICS (Brazil-Russia-India-China-South

Africa) development bank where Western influence presumably would not reach, as is the case with the World Bank.[20]

As a result of the Ukraine crisis, Russia's economic relations with the West, previously long thought to be a major requirement for growth and sustainable development of the Russian economy, have undergone a rapid turn-around. After nearly two decades spent negotiating and eventually winning the much sought-after membership in the World Trade Organization (WTO), which was supposed to mark a new stage in Russia's integration in the world economy, Russia is turning toward autarky as a hedge against Western politically-driven pressure. After committing to strengthen bilateral economic relations as ballast against political and geopolitical turbulence at the 2012 Los Cabos meeting of Presidents Obama and Putin, Russia is looking for ways to limit its exposure to U.S. economic influence.[21] The ultimate symbol of that shift was Prime Minister Dmitry Medvedev's support for legislation to empower the government to confiscate foreign property in Russia in retribution for Western sanctions.[22] Throughout his four-year term as president, Medvedev was known as an advocate of greater foreign investment in Russia as a means of modernizing and diversifying its economy. After acceding to the "reset" of U.S.-Russian relations in 2009—whose main theme was modernization of the Russian economy with the help of U.S. technology, know how, and investment—Russia is looking for ways to minimize its exposure to the West.

The need for such diversification and modernization was demonstrated when oil prices declined in the fall of 2014. Falling oil prices were widely seen as having far greater impact on the Russian economy than any of the sanctions imposed on Russia by the West. "Russia 2015: The Scenario Couldn't Be Worse," read the headline in a leading Russian newspaper, projecting a 1.5–2 percent decline in the GDP and a 9 percent drop in investment.[23]

It remains to be seen how successful the Russian government will be in devising, implementing, and sustaining this new course of self-reliance and isolation from the West. It is fraught with technological, financial, and political challenges for Russia, which in the quarter century of its post-Soviet existence has come to rely on Western technology and know-how, Western imports of equipment, services, and consumer goods, and Western financing. At the beginning of 2014, Russian corporations and banks were estimated to have some $550 billion in foreign debts.[24] Russian consumers have become accustomed to driving foreign cars and purchasing foreign-made goods. Russian airlines fly Boeings and Airbuses. And Russian tourists take it for granted that they can spend their summer holidays or winter breaks abroad. How far Russian autarky will go will almost certainly be a function of the severity and scope of Western sanctions. But for the Russian elite, the crisis in Ukraine has underscored the dangers of economic reliance on the West in an environment of major, fundamental political and geopolitical differences with it.

The Quest for a New Ideological Foundation

The Ukraine crisis and the rift with the West have created demands for a new ideological foundation for the Kremlin's course in the international arena. The two most prominent ideological currents to emerge from the crisis have been Eurasianism and the concept of the Russian World, akin to but less ambitious than the idea of Pan-Slavism that gained prominence in nineteenth-century Russia and provided a rationale for Russia to act as a gatherer of Slavic lands. Neither Eurasianism nor the

Russian World is new; both have deep roots in Russian intellectual history, and both underwent a renaissance after the dissolution of the Soviet Union when the new Russian state began its search for post-Soviet ideological mileposts to guide its foreign policy. Until recently, however, both had been relegated to the margins of the political and ideological conversation in Russia as the Kremlin pursued a course that, despite occasional detours, was for the most part Western-bound and dedicated to building closer relations with Europe and the United States.

The Ukraine crisis has changed that. At the very least it represents a major detour from the course Russia had been on for the previous quarter century. At most, it is truly a turning point that marks the beginning of a protracted break with the West comparable in many ways, albeit probably not in scope, to the Cold War.

Both Eurasianism and the Russian World provide reliable ideological foundations for those who argue that Russia represents a civilization that is separate and distinct from Europe and should be following its own path of domestic development and its own course in the international arena. With the crisis in Ukraine, both ideologies have moved considerably closer to the mainstream of the national discourse. Some of this newfound prominence owes, no doubt, to the Kremlin's desire to offer a sound justification for the shift in its policy that the rift with the West represents, but these ideologies' enduring presence in the country's national discourse points to the existence of a receptive audience for them in Russia.

Contemporary Russian Eurasianism derives in large measure from the writings of Lev Gumilev, a twentieth-century scholar who argued that Russia represents a separate civilization that does not belong to Europe and is instead a product of the

Mongolian occupation of Russia (which he considered benefi-
cial to Russia) in the thirteenth century, which lasted for some
250 years and resulted in a special relationship between Slavic
and Turkic peoples.[25] These ideas and their modern interpretations include the rejection of the Western liberal order and
advocacy of a Eurasian empire that, far from draining Russia's
resources—a point made by Aleksandr Solzhenitsyn among
others—will serve as the source of its strength and return to
greatness.[26]

The leading proponent of Eurasianism ideas in Russia today
is Aleksandr Dugin, whom we will encounter again, briefly, later
in this book. Long known for advocating Eurasianism, return
to the empire, and rejection of Western liberalism and U.S.-led
Atlanticism, Dugin, until recently, had remained on the margins of the policy and intellectual discussion in Russia. But the
crisis in Ukraine and the annexation of Crimea have propelled
Dugin and his associates to the leading ranks of the new, muscu-
lar brand of Russian foreign and security policy ideologues. They
argue for further expansion into Ukraine.[27]

The Russian World idea has gained prominence in Russian
discourse as an argument for the annexation of Crimea, for keeping Ukraine within Russia's orbit, and for supporting the separatist cause in Eastern Ukraine.[28] Ill-defined geographically and
politically, the Russian World is best described as a civilizational
concept in addition to a collection of territories and countries
populated by ethnic Russians or areas where Russian language
and culture play a prominent role in the life of the local population.[29] It is arguably a more assertive version of the long-standing theme in Russian foreign policy of protecting the rights of
fellow Russians and Russian speakers abroad, especially in the
territories of the former USSR. Western values and Western

liberal traditions are viewed by exponents of the Russian World idea as at best false and alien to it and at worst hostile to it.[30] Putin's speech announcing the annexation of Crimea effectively embraced the idea of the Russian World as one of the drivers of Russian foreign policy.[31]

A New Chapter of An Old Policy

In foreign policy, the Ukraine crisis reinforced the prevailing narrative in Russia that during the first decade of its post-Soviet existence the country had been too weak to stand up for its interests in the face of the West's encroachment. According to this reasoning, Russia's political and economic stabilization at the turn of the century—with the ascent of Putin to the presidency and a long period of robust economic growth—has enabled it to regain some of its military potential and a good deal of its international influence and has positioned it to push back against the West.[32] It was a narrative in which the West acted as an expansionist geopolitical actor whose hegemonic ambitions could be resisted only by a firm—and, if necessary, forceful—resistance.

Putin's 2007 speech at the Munich security conference and the war with Georgia in 2008 were intended to both punish Russia's small neighbor for seeking closer ties to the West and to send a strong signal to the West. Russia, in that message, would not tolerate interference in its zone of "privileged interests," let alone permit NATO expansion in the former Soviet states. According to this logic, the annexation of Crimea and the ongoing conflict in eastern Ukraine are both part of the same progression of Russian foreign policy following its recovery from the horrible decade of the 1990s, a policy designed and implemented to keep Ukraine out of NATO and NATO out of Ukraine.

The war with Georgia in 2008 had marked the first time in decades—since the 1979 Soviet invasion of Afghanistan—that Russia used military force against another independent, sovereign state. It shocked Europe, where the idea of partnership with Russia and non-use of force between states had taken hold after the end of the Cold War, and where both Georgia and Russia had been involved to varying degrees in a cooperative relationship with NATO. However, as an early warning of Russian intentions, the war with Georgia did not have quite the effect it was intended to have. As a first of its kind, it could be viewed as an aberration, a product of tensions between Russia and Georgia, and a result of Georgian miscalculation and provocative behavior. In the end, the war was not overlooked, but the West and Russia quickly moved past it in a new effort to patch up relations and rebuild cooperation deemed important for both sides.[33]

Following the war in Georgia, Russia consolidated its hold on breakaway Abkhazia and South Ossetia. Both territories took the symbolic step of declaring their independence from Georgia, thus signaling that there would be no way back, and Russia recognized them as sovereign, independent states. However, in an apparent token gesture of respect for the post–World War II international order, Russia did not annex South Ossetia and Abkhazia. An outright annexation of the two territories by Russia would have undermined their claims to the right of self-determination, as well as Russia's claim—no matter how unconvincing—that it had fought the war to protect its independence-bound clients against Georgian aggression.[34]

In the case of Crimea there was no attempt to maintain the pretense of the peninsula's independence. Moreover, while using the rationale of defending co-ethnics in the Russian World persecuted by a hostile regime, the Kremlin went further. It offered an additional justification for its action when it argued that it was not merely motivated by the obligation to defend compatriots, but that it was also acting to correct a historical injustice perpetrated during the tenure of Nikita Khrushchev who had given Crimea—an indisputably Russian territory—to Ukraine in 1954.

The annexation of Crimea marked the Kremlin's abandonment not only of the post–Cold War security order among the former Soviet states, whose leaders had agreed to recognize and respect their intra-USSR administrative boundaries as interstate borders, but also of the post–World War II European norms codified in the Helsinki Accords of 1975, which asserted the commitment of all European nations to recognize each other's borders and not change them by force.

For approximately two decades now, Russia's policy toward the West has been marked by internal consistency, growing increasingly confrontational as more resources have been put at its disposal. From declaratory opposition to NATO enlargement and Putin's Munich speech, to the war with Georgia and the annexation of Crimea, Russian resistance to perceived Western encroachment has progressed from words to deeds. Consistent as it is, this chain of Russian policy responses leaves open the question of whether the annexation of Crimea was the result of a deliberate strategy or a panicky response to an unexpected crisis. The response was new, unprecedented, and unpredicted, but it fell within the familiar pattern of Russian foreign policy when its leadership was challenged with new circumstances that neither they nor anyone in the West had likely foreseen.

What Will the Neighbors Say?

Besides opening a new chapter in Russia's relations with the West, the Ukraine crisis has marked a new stage in its dealings with its closest neighbors—the states of the former Soviet Union. Their relationship has been complicated since the moment of the dissolution of the Soviet Union, burdened by mutual dependencies, mistrust, competing interests, and difficult legacies.

Whereas some Soviet republics were eager to leave the USSR behind—Ukraine among them—others were ambivalent about it. For many of these republics about to become independent states, the prospect of independence was welcome on the one hand as a step toward national self-fulfillment, but troublesome on the other hand, because of their economic, political, and social ties to and dependence on Russia. This ambivalence has remained an important feature of their relations to the present day.

Although all ex-Soviet states want to be free to pursue their independent domestic and foreign policies, most, if not all, are to some degree dependent on Russia's good will. For some, such as Kazakhstan where ethnic Russians still account for a quarter of the population, maintaining good relations and economic and political ties with Russia is a matter of national survival.[35] For others, such as Tajikistan—impoverished, lacking the oil and gas resources of Kazakhstan, and facing an unstable neighbor in Afghanistan—Russia is a source of as much as half of GDP, largely derived from remittances sent by laborers working in Russia. For Belarus, a beneficiary of Russian subsidies in the form of cheap gas, cheap oil, and cheap loans, the relationship with Russia is also key. For Armenia, with historical enemies Turkey and Azerbaijan on most of its borders, Russia is a source of strategic reassurance, security, and economic assistance.

Russian assertiveness appears to be a problem for many. Armenia had been negotiating its own AA and DCFTA with the EU, but under Russian pressure was forced to shift course and agree to join the CU.[36] Kazakhstan has joined the CU but has bristled at its terms and the consequences of joining it.[37] Kyrgyzstan has promised to join in 2015 but warned that it would not comply with its terms until 2020.[38] Even Belarus, which is Russia's sole partner in the so-called union state and depends heavily on Moscow's largess for economic sustenance, has managed to resist Russian pressure. Following Ukraine's signing of the AA and DCFTA with the EU, Belarus, joined by Kazakhstan, refused Russian demands to restrict Ukrainian exports.[39]

Unable to deflect Russian pressure, none of the former Soviet states is likely to harbor illusions about the true motives of Moscow's integrationist drive and the consequences for them. Close economic and political ties with Russia are a necessity for many leaders of these countries, who either need cheap Russian gas sold at a special discount to customs union members, or, ostracized in the West for undemocratic practices, rely on Russia for political support, or as in the case of Armenia, see in Russia the necessary geopolitical partner in a tough neighborhood. A bad relationship with Russia is not an option for them.[40] But the crisis in Ukraine, the annexation of Crimea, and the separatist conflict in eastern Ukraine will no doubt feed resentment of Russia and its policies among its vulnerable neighbors and push them to hedge against further Russian moves.[41]

China—Ties that Bind

"China Concentrates the Mind," wrote Dmitri Trenin well over a decade ago.[42] Russian-Chinese relations have been improving steadily for the past quarter century. In 2008, the two countries finalized their border treaty, settling their long-running territorial disputes. China has become Russia's largest trading partner; the volume of their bilateral trade is set to reach $100 billion in 2015. Putin and Xi Jinping have exchanged symbolically important first foreign visits to each other's country upon taking office. The two countries appear to coordinate closely their positions in the Security Council. And in the midst of the Ukraine crisis, amid calls for international isolation of Russia, Putin was received with open arms in Beijing and signed a long-awaited gas deal with China. On the surface, things couldn't be better between the two neighbors.

However, the rapprochement between China and Russia is only half the story. The complete story would include the fact that it took well over a decade after the relationship between the two neighbors was normalized to finalize their border agreement. It took ten years to negotiate the massive gas deal, the terms of which have not been made public.[43] There were discussions among leading Russian foreign policy minds, demographers, economists, and journalists about the risk of losing Siberia and the Far East to China.[44] There were also Russian concerns about growing Chinese military might and the danger of Chinese expansion.[45] In short, a full account of the state and direction of Russian-Chinese relations reflects the Russian foreign policy and national security community's profound discomfort with the unequal relationship between the two giant neighbors—discomfort arising from fears about the rise of China and the challenge it poses to Russia.

The Ukraine crisis is likely to amplify that challenge. The rift between Russia and the West—already deep, highly unlikely to be healed in the foreseeable future and only promising to get even deeper—leaves Russia with few partners abroad. NATO and the EU are not seeking to expand the confrontation with Russia, but any talk about a rapprochement or partnership has been shelved. The trade and economic relationship will continue as a matter of necessity, but without any illusions that trade and economic relations can lead to closer political relations. Moreover, the crisis has highlighted as never before Europe's dependence on Russian gas and has spurred a new round of discussions in Europe and in the United States about diversifying Europe's energy supply and making it less dependent on Russia.

The rift between Russia and the West has underscored the importance for Russia of its relations with China. Western sanctions, and the threat of more to come, have highlighted for Russia its dependence on Europe and the United States for markets for its exports, as well as for key sources of capital and important technologies. For Russia, that relationship is a source not only of leverage, but also of vulnerability.

But despite the apparent economic complementarity between Russia and China—China is resource-hungry, Russia is resource-rich—Moscow views growing reliance on Beijing as fraught with new challenges. Instead of expanding the Kremlin's room for maneuvering, further reliance on China could end up shrinking it. According to Russian leaders, the gas deal signed by Russia and China during Putin's visit to Beijing in May 2014 took a decade to negotiate because of China's exceedingly difficult—and undisclosed—terms, as well as its unwillingness to yield. While the pipeline deal will finally provide an opening for Russian gas to the Asia-Pacific market, it has been widely seen as a victory for China, which took advantage of Russia's estrangement from the West and forced Putin to agree to a deal that was criticized even in Russia as unfavorable.[46]

Frictions over gas prices are but one example of the tension between Russia and China. The two countries' competition in Central Asia, where China has rapidly overshadowed Russia in trade and investment, is another.[47] The Ukraine crisis offered a third: rather than side with Russia in the Security Council, China abstained on the resolution condemning the annexation of Crimea, leaving Moscow to cast the sole veto. Moscow's disregard for the principle of sovereignty and territorial integrity has no doubt made it uncomfortable for Beijing, acutely sensitive to these two issues for its own reasons, to endorse the annexation of Crimea.[48] This follows China's similar response to the 2008 Russian war with Georgia and the declaration of independence by Abkhazia and South Ossetia, neither of which Beijing has recognized.[49]

In the near term, the gas deal with China, symbolic of the improving relationship with Beijing, enables Moscow to demonstrate to the West that it has options elsewhere. However, if, as is likely to be the case, the Ukraine crisis only deepens estrangement from the West over the long term, closer Russian ties to China are likely to prove binding rather than liberating for Russia.

A Military Renaissance

One of the greatest surprises of the Ukraine crisis has been the performance of the Russian military. Since the late 1980s, and especially during the 1990s, the once formidable Russian military machine came to be seen as a pale shadow of its former self, a broken, underfinanced, undermanned organization known more for its blunders and cruel treatment of recruits than for success on the battlefield.[50] Even the brief and victorious 2008 war with Georgia, much celebrated in Russia, served as a reminder of the many shortcomings of the Russian military.

The war with Georgia, while demonstrating Russian resolve to use military force in defense of its interests around its periphery, highlighted the need and set the stage for far-reaching military reform. Over the next five years, the size of the armed forces was cut from 1.2 million to 1 million. The hollow structure of skeleton divisions to be activated and manned in the event of a major war, along with many senior and general officer billets, was eliminated, with the officer corps cut by as much as 50 percent. Defense spending went up year after year. The armed forces' pay improved; they received new equipment and more and better training. An ambitious decade-long $700 billion defense modernization program was launched.[51] The Russian military was transformed, even more so in image than in substance, but the image it projected during the Ukraine crisis of a well-oiled military machine helped burnish its new credentials as a force to be reckoned with.

The new Russian military is still a far cry from the old Soviet-era military institution. It is only a fraction of its former self, and even in its much reduced size it appears to be a challenge for the country to man properly: the demographic base has shrunk, and the budget is not sufficient to recruit enough professional soldiers and pay them enough to make military service attractive. Technologically, the armed forces will continue to face significant challenges as domestic weapons manufacturers have suffered from many years of underinvestment, especially during the lean 1990s. The push to import military technology and equipment under the previous Defense Minister Anatoliy Serdyukov has ground to a halt under pressure from domestic manufacturers and also as a result of Western sanctions.[52]

On several occasions throughout the Ukraine crisis, Russia has deployed large military formations on the border with Ukraine. The move generated considerable alarm in Ukraine and in the West and fears of a military invasion. However, the 40,000-strong military formation is unlikely to be a sufficient force for a full-scale military invasion and occupation of Ukraine. More likely, it is better suited for a limited incursion designed to reinforce the separatists in eastern Ukrainian enclaves and create a permanent frozen conflict under the guise of a peacekeeping operation. However, even such a relatively limited incursion is likely to tax the capabilities of the Russian military in the event of a protracted occupation and a related counterinsurgency campaign. (The additional forces required for this mission would have to be drawn from units dedicated to other regions and missions in the North Caucasus and Central Asia.) Neither of these would pose an immediate risk to Russian security, but a protracted operation could.[53]

Perhaps more important than the size and the quality of its armed forces, Russia has demonstrated not only its ability, but also its will to use force against its neighbors and against perceived Western challenges to its security interests. Having done so, it has re-established itself as the superior military force on the territory of the former Soviet Union. This victory, however, has come at a price, manifested in new estrangement from the West, an increasingly challenging relationship with China, and a hollow partnership with the immediate neighbors in the former USSR.

Russia after the Ukraine Crisis

While the Ukraine crisis has accelerated existing trends in Russian domestic development and foreign and security policy, it did not give rise to them. But it does represent a major turning point that will affect Russia both domestically and internationally. The long-standing and interrelated themes of international integration and domestic modernization have little relevance to today's Russia and are unlikely to regain relevance in the foreseeable future. The Ukraine crisis has put Russia on the path of significant international isolation with few allies and partners; those allies that Russia does have are mostly states that in one way or another are dependent on it.

Russia's willingness to use force against and annex a major territory belonging to one of its neighbors represents a major departure from the declaratory policy of the Russian Federation throughout much of the post–Cold War era. Opposition to the United States—viewed as a revisionist power violating the sovereignty of other states by interfering in their internal affairs—has been a staple of Russian foreign policy. Yet Russia has abandoned its adherence to that principle, becoming a revisionist power in its own right.

Russia is paying a heavy price for its victory in Crimea and for what gains it may have achieved by keeping Ukraine in its orbit. Indeed, those gains may very well prove illusory, while the toll on Russia—political, economic, military, and reputational—is bound to be heavy and lasting.

4   Europe and the Crisis

We turn now to Europe, taking the EU and NATO as frames of reference. The former allows for an examination of Europe's role in political and economic terms, the latter for considering the military and security aspects of European policy. Of course, the two organizations are not monoliths, and certainly were not during the Ukraine crisis. There were differences within the EU, just as there have been within NATO (both among Europeans and between them and the United States), not least because policies toward Ukraine are inseparable from Europe's and America's relationship with Russia. Hence the Ukraine crisis also offers an opportunity to assess the transatlantic relationship, and NATO's future in particular.

The EU's Allure

By the time the USSR disintegrated, Europe had been transformed, in no small measure because of the remarkable achievements of the EU. In the three centuries prior to initiation of regional integration in Europe in the 1950s, war among European states remained a constant threat, if only because it had erupted so regularly. Once the seedlings of what would become the EU were planted in the 1950s, a major war among the European states that constituted the coalition had already become all but impossible—no small feat given the wars they had fought over the past several centuries. In short, a continent of war had metamorphosed into a community of peace, and did so within a generation.[1]

The process that produced this outcome, which approximated the Kantian vision of a "perpetual peace," was hard fought and risked failure because it required revolutionary decisions: the abolition of internal tariffs, the adoption of a common external tariff, the coordination of national policies on numerous issues, and the creation of European institutions with substantial supranational powers. Thanks to the attractiveness of these achievements, the six pioneers of European integration—Belgium, France, Germany, Luxembourg, Italy, and the Netherlands—had become a club of twelve by the time the Cold War ended. During the 1990s, the EU would add three more members: Austria, Finland, and Sweden. More dramatically, it established a single currency (the euro, introduced in 2002) and central bank (and thus a shared monetary policy, encompassing members of the Eurozone), reached the Schengen Agreement on passport-free travel among a subset of its members, and started work on common foreign and security policies.

A new political formation had arisen in Europe, one that banished the blight of war, secured democracy and prosperity, and forced a rethinking of received conceptions of sovereignty. Little wonder, then, that the EU was a club the former communist states of East-Central Europe and the most democratized former Soviet republics—the Baltic states—were keen to join. The EU, for its part, encouraged their quest for membership—subject to advances in building democracy, good governance, and market economies—because it seemed an effective way to help them navigate the passage from Soviet-style socialism to democratic capitalism. In 2004, in its single largest expansion to date, the EU took in eight Central European countries: the Czech Republic, Estonia, Latvia, Lithuania, Hungary, Poland, Slovakia, and Slovenia (plus Malta and Cyprus). With the admission of Romania and Bulgaria in 2007, it reached the current tally of twenty-eight. Additional candidates waited in the wings, and the door is open for former Soviet republics to increase ties with the EU on various fronts and perhaps even to gain admittance.[2]

The EU's eastward extension raised the question of what its policy ought to be toward former Soviet republics that were not members, and perhaps would never be, but had become the EU's next-door neighbors following the 2004 enlargement. This marked a contrast from prior years when the EU had focused largely on East-Central Europe. The consensus in Brussels became that initiatives ought to be developed for working with the EU's new eastern neighbors on a wide front: market reform, democratization, effective governance, the promotion of civil society, human rights, police and military reform, environmental protection, and energy efficiency and security. The EU countries geographically closest to the former Soviet states naturally had the biggest stake in this planned partnership. They believed that their own security, democracy, and prosperity were tied to the success of political and economic reform in the states on their eastern flank and that the hope of EU membership, and in the meantime the reality of systematic cooperation, could encourage and assist their efforts.

The EU Looks East

Two programs were central to the EU's eastern outreach. The first, the European Neighborhood Policy (ENP), was established in 2004 and encompassed sixteen Middle Eastern and post-Soviet states.[3] The second, the Eastern Policy (EaP), was focused on Armenia, Belarus, Azerbaijan, Georgia, Moldova, and Ukraine.[4] Ukraine was only one of the six countries covered by the EaP, but it was the priority from the outset. That status owed to Ukraine's size and the fact that it bridges the EU and Russia and abuts four EU states: Poland, Slovakia, Hungary, and Romania. Of these, Poland was particularly keen on the EaP's success. As we discussed in in the first chapter, Poles have strong historical connections, though a complicated and not always amicable history, with Ukrainians and have been at war with, or under the occupation of, Russia (in its tsarist and Soviet incarnations) several times since the seventeenth century. Unsurprisingly, Poland, together with Sweden, the EaP's intellectual progenitor, regarded Ukraine as a bulwark against Russia. And by extension, it considered Ukraine the program's keystone, the more so following the 2004–2008 "color revolutions" in Georgia, Kyrgyzstan, and Ukraine, and the 2008 Russia-Georgia war, which highlighted Russia's resurgence and its neighbors' fragility, but also their democratic potential.[5]

The concept of an Association Agreement (AA) flowed from the EaP's basic aims. It was conditional on an EaP member's progress in implementing economic and political reforms related to democracy, human rights, and markets and was conceived as a bilateral accord that would be tailored to an individual state's circumstances and offer assorted opportunities for integration. While EU membership was not integral to the EaP, neither was it foreclosed. This doubtless reflected a compromise between the EU states that most favored expansion (those in East-Central Europe and the Baltics) and those that did not (much of the rest of the EU) and were also more mindful of Moscow's suspicions that the EaP, its benign mission statement notwithstanding, would inevitably erode Russia's influence in its immediate neighborhood and was in fact intended to do just that.[6]

The benefits that the EaP offered included easier, less expensive visas to EU countries (with the view of eventually allowing visa-free visits for ninety days), duty-free access for exports to the EU's massive market, and assistance for improving energy and transportation infrastructure and education. The negotiations for an AA with Ukraine—which included a Deep and Comprehensive Free Trade Area (DCFTA)—preceded the EaP itself and occurred between 2007 and 2011. The EU and Ukraine initialed the text in 2012, a prelude to signature, or so it was believed. While there was uncertainty, indeed skepticism, among European leaders about Yanukovych's commitment to enacting the AA-mandated reforms, as the November 2013 EaP summit in Vilnius neared, he was expected to sign it.

Europe and the Rebellion

Facing a mix of Russian pressure (barriers against Ukrainian exports and intimations of increased gas prices) and inducements (promises of a large loan and a cut in gas prices), Yanukovych iced the AA at the Vilnius conclave. When he visited Moscow the following month, Putin offered him big carrots in recompense: a $15 billon loan, in the form of bond purchases; a reduction, as a stopgap measure, of about $150 in the price that Ukraine paid per thousand cubic meters of Russian gas, a one-third reduction estimated to yield Ukraine another $3.5 billion; and the lifting of the barriers imposed on Ukrainian exports in order to pressure Kyiv prior to the Vilnius gathering.[7] As mentioned in the first chapter, the reforms required by the AA would have dismantled the crooked house that Yanukovych and his predecessors, Kuchma above all, had built. That explains why Yanukovych dissembled on enacting them, dithered on signing the accord, and refused to comply with Europe's demand that Tymoshenko be freed. Putin's Russia, by contrast, was prepared to offer economic help without asking for the pesky reforms that the EU required and that threatened the foundation of the house of Yanukovych and the lifestyles of its most privileged inhabitants. This last consideration, as we also observed in the first chapter, was arguably more important than Russian pressure or blandishments because it turned on the supreme imperative of self-and system-protection.

When Yanukovych finally decided to mothball the accord, it appeared that Putin had prevailed and that Yanukovych would formally and definitively abandon the AA and instead attach Ukraine to the Russian-led Customs Union, of which Belarus and Kazakhstan were already members. But as we have noted in previous chapters, once news of his decision broke, Yanukovych was besieged by massive street protests, their epicenter in central and western Ukraine—the strongholds of support for alignment with the West and antipathy toward his government. Kyiv became the focal point of this revolt, its streets and Independence Square (Maidan) overflowing with demonstrators, evoking memories of the Orange Revolution. Yanukovych unleashed his riot police to quell the crowds, but that move led to fatalities that mounted steadily and enraged the opposition.

Amidst the melee, EU emissaries tried to nudge him toward a compromise with the opposition, while Russia urged him to stand firm. But the demonstrators were relentless and unbowed, and the death toll rose as their clashes with the riot police continued. February proved a bloody month: between the 17th and 21st alone 100 people were killed.[8] Even before then, however, it was evident that Yanukovych was a leader living on borrowed time. The protests, ignited by his backsliding on the AA, had transformed from rallies powered by disgust over corruption into a campaign aimed at overthrowing the government.

Defections from his regime mounted. His oligarchical allies began to hedge their bets and focus on their long-term survival. A power-sharing accord mediated by EU leaders, signed on February 21 between Yanukovych and key opposition leaders, failed to find favor among the protestors and hardline opposition figures.[9] His dwindling political capital depleted, Yanukovych fled on February 22, and the parliament voted to oust his government and to release Tymoshenko. The upshot was that what the EU lacked in strategy for countering Russian resistance to a consummation of EaP-derived agreements was provided by the Ukrainian street.

The Toothless EaP

The rebellion triggered by Yanukovych's decision on the AA—and, more broadly, by simmering discontent over the authoritarianism and corruption that marked his regime—revealed a major weakness of the EaP. Its premise, even if implicit, was that Russia would somehow accept, even if not gracefully, the integration of post-Soviet states into the EU, and indeed that it would have no choice but to come to terms with that denouement, despite finding it disagreeable. There was little basis for such a rosy assumption, however, given the importance that Russia attaches to Ukraine for historical, economic, cultural, and strategic reasons.

Besides, Putin and senior members of his government had long been leery of the EaP and had openly attacked it as a device designed to intrude into areas that adjoined Russia and were vital to its security and standing.[10] The EU presented the EaP as high-minded venture aimed at promoting prosperity and stability to the benefit of all, Russia included, but that was not how it was seen in Moscow. To the Russian leadership, it was a maneuver to expand the West's sphere of influence—in other words, of a piece with the (successful) Western-backed anti-regime movements in Georgia (2003), Ukraine (2004), and Kyrgyzstan (2006). Indeed Putin characterized the EaP as a complement to NATO.[11] Moscow had moved even before this to build its own Eurasian bloc to stymie what it considered Western efforts to undercut Russia in adjoining and proximate regions. The Russia-Belarus-Kazakhstan Eurasian Customs Union had been established in 2010, and the Kremlin was keen on Ukraine and other former Soviet states signing on. That organization was complemented by plans for a Eurasian Economic Union, and the trio signed the underlying treaty in May 2014.

So Russia's opposition to the EaP was not just verbal; it had taken countermeasures. As two European scholars observed about the EaP:

> Moscow does not view the increasing influence of the EU in its immediate proximity as a win-win situation because it brings democracy and stability, but rather as a loss of power and influence. It is of no use to repeat continuously the empty claim that Russia benefits from this

> development. It is much more important to integrate Rus-
> sia into concrete projects in the region.[12]

But of course in the minds of the EaP's most fervent promoters it was meant precisely to exclude Russia, not integrate it.

During the Russia-Georgia war of 2008, Putin had successfully tested the will of the EU and NATO. His goal was to demonstrate through Georgia's defeat that Russia would not forfeit its historic predominance in its periphery. To make the same point through economic means, in the run-up to the EaP's Vilnius summit he dogged Armenia into dropping its plan to sign an AA and to join the Customs Union instead and blocked Ukrainian goods from Russian markets, along with Moldova's wine exports. (He did not succeed fully: Moldova, along with Georgia, initialed the AA at Vilnius and, together with post-Yanukovych Ukraine, signed it on June 27, 2014.[13])

In short, the EU had good reason, based on the Kremlin's words and deeds, to expect that Moscow would resist EaP initiatives that threatened to draw Ukraine away from Russia. But when the resistance became reality in 2014, Europe was largely helpless, just as it was in Georgia in 2008.

Moscow's Apprehensions

There were several reasons that Moscow was determined to counter the EU's increasing influence in the post-Soviet states generally and the EaP and the accompanying AA/DCTA in particular.[14]

First, the EU had become an increasingly important source of trade and investment for several countries that Russia regards as constituting its extended neighborhood. Russia remained Ukraine's largest individual trade partner in 2014—with total trade amounting to $12.6 billion, or 27 percent of Ukraine's exports and

30 percent of its imports—but by then Ukraine was conducting a slightly larger proportion of its overall trade with the EU bloc.[15] In Moscow's eyes, the AA would have accelerated this trend, making Ukraine less dependent on Russia for goods, technology, and capital, and increasing the role of Europe, which simply had more to offer as a market and a source of investment and technology than the Russian economy, whose mainstay is energy. The inevitable result would have been reduced Russian influence, and not just economic, in a critical neighboring country. Putin declared in 2013 that the EU-Ukraine trade deal presented a "big threat" to Russia because EU goods would make their way into Russia's market from Ukraine given the free-trade arrangement between Moscow and Kyiv and that Russia's agriculture and its automotive industries would be "choked as a result."[16] But ultimately his apprehensions were not limited to trade competition; they reflected Russia's concerns about a general loss of influence in its most strategically significant neighbor.

Second, though the AA does not provide Ukraine—or any other EaP participant—assurance of EU membership, Russia could not exclude the possibility that a future Ukrainian government would make enough progress in implementing the AA/DCFTA-mandated reforms to qualify as a candidate member, a position that would make full membership realistic down the road. This fear was not necessarily far-fetched; after all, there was a time when Romania's and Bulgaria's chances for joining the EU seemed slim. So it was scarcely unrealistic for Putin to assume that Ukraine could prove to be another dark horse that defied the odds.

Third, even as a non-member of the EU, Ukraine could, like Serbia, join the organization's Energy Community and then implement the accompanying regulations. Of these, the one most vexing to Moscow is the Third Energy Package (TEP), which was proposed by the EU Commission in 2007 and took effect in the fall of 2009.[17] In essence, TEP's purpose is to increase competition in the EU's energy market in order to reduce Europe's exposure to political pressure from suppliers (Russia being the most important) and to obtain lower prices. To this end, the legislation bars companies (European and foreign) that extract energy used by EU consumers from also owning the distribution networks, pipelines being the most important component.

This stipulation has harmful ramifications for Russian energy companies that own energy deposits and are also in the business of extraction and distribution—Gazprom above all. For instance, TEP could block Russia's debt-for-equity proposals that have been aimed at enabling Gazprom to gain a stake in, or even full ownership of, Ukraine's pipeline and storage network. This was not a far-fetched concern. As it happened, in June 2014 the Secretariat of the EU Energy Community notified Ukraine, which by then had signed the AA, that the contract between Gazprom and Naftohaz, Ukraine's state-owned energy, contravened EU rules.[18] Compliance with TEP would require Gazprom to renegotiate agreements for pipeline projects in which it holds major stakes and that are intended to diversify Russian export routes to Europe, namely Nord Stream (Russia to EU markets via the Baltic Sea) and South Stream (Russia to EU consumers through the Black Sea and the Balkans). TEP had already become a testy matter between the EU and Russia; the latter, contending that it is illegal, took its case to the WTO in 2014. As the Kremlin saw it, the TEP could turn out to be but one of the EU standards that Ukraine could implement that would hurt Russia both economically and strategically.

Relatedly, in Moscow's mind there is a link between membership in the EU and membership in NATO. The two coalitions overlap substantially in membership—twenty-two out of twenty-eight EU members are in NATO—and present themselves as organizations committed to common values and indeed to a "strategic partnership" based on the 2002 "EU-NATO Declaration on a European Security and Defense Policy."[19] Even though membership in one does not guarantee membership in the other, Russia could not on that basis alone exclude the possibility that a Ukraine in the EU could eventually become a Ukraine in NATO. That prospect was not altogether fanciful; recall that Kuchma had declared in 2002 that Ukraine was ready to join NATO and that following the Orange Revolution the alliance's 2008 Bucharest summit declaration stated that "NATO welcomes Ukraine's and Georgia's Euro-Atlantic aspirations for membership in NATO. We agreed today that these countries will join NATO. . . . Today we make clear that we support these countries' application for MAP [Membership Action Plan]."[20] Why would a Ukrainian government that had integrated extensively with the EU not be in a strong position for NATO membership, and why would it not work hard to make the case that it was? From Moscow's standpoint, then, if the AA were to increase the chances, however slim they might have appeared in 2014, of Ukraine joining the EU, it could also make Ukraine's admittance into NATO more probable.

Finally, Ukraine's accession to the AA mattered to Moscow because it portended a potential parting of ways between Russia and Ukraine in a cultural-civilizational sense. It is easy to dismiss this factor given the prevailing tendency in contemporary political analyses to conceptualize wins and losses, threats and opportunities, in tangible, and preferably numerical, form. But that which cannot be touched or counted is not necessarily less important to states, and the historical survey in Chapter 1 provides ample grounds for taking account of it in understanding Russian policies toward Ukraine.

Certainly, what animates far-right Russian nationalists, such as Aleksandr Prokhanov and Aleksandr Dugin—who have demanded an aggressive defense of Russian interests in Ukraine and even criticized Putin for not providing it—is not the prospect of commercial losses to the West in Ukraine as a result of the AA. To them, the competition over Ukraine—whether in the form of the EaP, the AA/DCFTA, or NATO's Partnership for Peace, to say nothing of membership in the alliance—constitutes a particular instance of a larger campaign that the liberal Euro-Atlantic coalition has conducted since the Cold War to undo Russia's historic primacy in adjacent countries by shaping people's ways of thinking and being and reaping the strategic gains that follow from that success.[21] While this ideological strain, and others inspired by Eurasianism, which presents Russia as the center of a civilization distinct from Western liberalism, does not by itself determine Russian foreign policy, neither is it devoid of influence within Russia's governing institutions, and on Putin himself.[22]

EU Options

The EU was not oblivious to these various concerns of Moscow's. But it was also determined that awareness of them not lead to a legitimation of what president Dmitry Medvedev referred to, following the 2008 war with Georgia, as Russia's "privileged interests" in the post-Soviet states.[23] Moreover, it rejected Russia's claim that the EaP was nothing but an old-fashioned quest for a sphere of influence clad in the fashionable garb of regional economic cooperation. Yet Brussels appears to have given little thought, if any at all, to how it would deal with the eventuality of Russian resistance—a curious failure considering how unlikely it is that a great power would passively accept the attrition of its predominance in areas vital to its prestige and security and trust in the reassuring rhetoric of its rivals. There was no reason to believe, particularly after its war with Georgia, that Russia would be an exception; Putin's decision to respond to Yanukovych's ouster by annexing Crimea and backing Donbas separatists proved that it was not.

The EU could not, of course, counter Putin's moves in Ukraine militarily. For one thing, it lacks the capacity: few of its members spend substantially on their armed forces and, in any event, the EU was not under any obligation to protect EaP members given that the program makes no security commitments. Besides, not even Russia's toughest critics in the United States, let alone the White House, were calling for the use of force, which, it was clear to all, would have created a far more dangerous crisis. And military options had even less appeal among European leaders, to say nothing of the general public. The only feasible means available to the EU, therefore, was diplomatic and economic pressure. But when it came to the operational details of even these two options—what should be done, by whom, when, to what degree, and at what cost—there were no agreed-upon answers within Europe.

There were three reasons for the lack of clarity. First, the EU has long struggled to reach consensus when confronted with high-stakes controversies, internal and external, the more so as its membership has expanded. Second, the most influential EU members (Britain, France, Italy, and Germany) have substantial and lucrative economic ties with Russia—a point discussed later in this chapter—and are also less exposed to its power than are the EU's East Central European members. The latter are weaker and also feel more vulnerable on account of their location and their historical memories of Imperial Russia and the Soviet Union. Third, because Europe conducts far more trade with Russia than does the United States, its exposure to negative economic consequences was greater. The result was a division within the EU, and between key EU states and Washington, on just how much political isolation and economic pressure Putin's Russia should be subjected to and how productive placing it under such duress would be.

No amount of spin from Brussels and Washington could disguise this discord, which manifested itself even when it came to symbolic pressure. Consider one example. As the Ukrainian crisis intensified, the West searched for ways to isolate Russia politically and symbolically. After some debate it was decided in March that Europe and the United States would boycott the June G-8 summit, which Putin was scheduled to host—Russia having joined the group in 1998—and in Sochi no less and that Russia's membership in the elite group should be suspended.[24] The remaining members of the club of economic powers—the original G-7—met without him, in Brussels, on June 4-5. But then came the June 6 ceremonies marking the seventieth anniversary of D-Day. The night before, French president François Hollande held two consecutive dinners, one with President Obama, the second with the Putin, with whom the American leader did not wish to dine or hold a formal meeting. British Prime Minister David Cameron arrived a day in advance of the festivities to meet Putin, and German Chancellor Angela Merkel met Putin in their aftermath.[25] British and German communications mavens got busy explaining why their leaders' meetings with Putin were actually a show of Western unity because they had pressed him to change his policies in in Ukraine. But that was not the way it was seen, in Russia or elsewhere, particularly because Canadian Prime Minister Stephen Harper and President Obama had specifically urged against meetings with Putin.[26]

Pressuring Putin: You First

By March, the EU had applied its initial sanctions on Russia, but the restrictions targeted individuals within Putin's circle, not key sectors of the Russian economy, and were widely seen as little more than a slap on the wrist. Only in July did the EU overcome its hesitation and divisions and tighten the screws significantly by going beyond sanctions against the Russian elite, targeting sectors of Russia's economy, and closing the gap between Europe and the United States. The stimulus for the sterner action was an unexpected and horrific event. On July 17, 298 people were killed when Malaysia Airlines Flight 17 (MH-17) was shot down in the airspace of eastern Ukraine by a surface-to-air-missile, which was almost certainly fired by anti-Kyiv rebels who, it was widely assumed, had received the weapon from Russia.

There are several reasons it took that terrible event to narrow the gap between the United States and the EU, and within Europe itself, on sanctions. There is, to begin with, the economic asymmetry between the EU and the United States on commercial transactions with Russia. The United States' trade with Russia in 2012 amounted to a mere $40 billion.[27] By contrast, EU-Russian trade for that year was $437 billion—more than ten times greater.[28] Furthermore, the EU economies are far more trade-dependent than the United States. For example, between

2009 and 2013, trade accounted for 23.9 percent of American GDP; the corresponding ratios for Belgium, the Netherlands, Germany, and France were significantly larger.[29]

Though Russia accounts for a relatively small percentage of most EU countries' total trade, its role is not trivial. While trade with Russia made up only 9.5 percent of total EU trade in 2013, Russia is the bloc's third most important partner. (The EU is Russia's leading trade partner, accounting for almost 50 percent of the total.)[30] Likewise, though Russia is not a top-tier trade partner for most EU countries, it placed 13th for Germany in 2013, and in 2011 it was 10th for France's imports and 9th for exports, 10th for Italy's exports and imports, and among Britain's top 15 trade partners.[31] And these figures obscure Russia's importance for European economies in certain individual sectors. The upshot of this asymmetry was that Europe was more vulnerable than the United States to a boomerang effect from sanctions.

European leaders were particularly sensitive to this given that their countries' economies remained stuck in the wake of the 2008 recession: in the second quarter of 2014, economic growth in the Eurozone countries averaged 0.2 percent, and the economies of Germany, France, and Italy contracted.[32] Even the German economy, which had served as a flagging Europe's locomotive, was in trouble: it contracted by 0.2 percent in the second quarter of 2014, and the growth forecast for the year was revised from 1.8 percent to 1.2 percent.[33] With Europe's sluggish growth rates came high unemployment: 11.5 percent in June 2014 in the Eurozone, 10.2 in the EU as a whole. And the situation was far worse among youth: 23.1 percent in the EU, 23.8 percent in the Eurozone, and below 19 percent in only 6 countries (Estonia, Malta, Denmark, the Netherlands, Austria, and Germany).[34]

When it comes to Russia's importance for specific economic sectors in Europe, energy is the most important. But the dependence is not limited to imports from Russia; in addition, Europe's biggest energy companies have lucrative business deals in Russia. The French oil giant Total has a joint venture with Russia's Lukoil to extract shale gas from the vast Bazhenov deposit in Siberia. British Petroleum has a 19.75 percent stake in Rosneft, Russia's biggest oil company. The investment of Germany's E.ON conglomerate totals nearly $8 billion, mainly in electricity networks. Outside the energy sector, Russian airlines have purchased 270 aircraft from Airbus since 1994. European agricultural and food exports to Russia, while they accounted for less than 10 percent of all EU exports to the Russia market, totaled $15.8 billion in 2013 compared to $1.3 billion in U.S. sales that year, with Germany, Poland, the Netherlands, France, Italy, and Spain accounting for the largest sales.[35] And this is just a sampling of Europe's business ties with Russia.

EU Trade with Russia (Billions of U.S. Dollars)						
Country	1996	2000	2004	2008	2012	2013
Austria	1.1	0.9	2.3	5.1	5.6	N/A
Belgium	2.7	2.4	6	13.6	18	22.3
Czech Republic	2.7	2.5	3.7	13.1	14	14.6
Denmark	1.1	0.8	1.8	3.6	2.9	4.4
Estonia	1.2	1	1.9	3.8	5.6	5.3
Finland	4.5	3.2	12	26	21	21
France	5.9	6	13	30.5	27.1	24.2
Germany	14.5	15.8	30	84	105	88.1
Hungary	2.8	3	4.3	14	11.6	12
Italy	N/A	5	14.3	29	36.4	41
Netherlands	3.3	3.9	11.4	28.7	36.4	N/A
Poland	4.2	5.4	9.2	29.5	29	36.1
Slovakia	N/A	2.2	3.1	10.4	11	11.6
Spain	2	2.8	5.7	15.3	14.1	14.7
Sweden	1.2	1.1	4	11.2	12.2	10.5
United Kingdom	3.3	4	9.7	20	24	18.7

Table 4.1

EU trade with Russia. Source: Organization for Economic Cooperation and Development (OECD), http://stats.oecd.org/Index.aspx?DatasetCode=HS1988#

As Table 4.1 shows, not all EU countries have substantial trade ties with Russia in dollar terms, though a number do, and the value has increased since the mid-1990s. For 2012, the latest year for which complete data is available, those that conduct significant trade with Russia included Belgium, the Czech Republic, France, Germany, Hungary, Italy, Poland, Slovakia, Spain, and the UK. Though European countries' economies are far smaller than the United States' (U.S. GDP was 4.5 times larger than that of Germany, Europe's economic powerhouse, in 2012), the value of Germany's trade with Russia was 2.5 times greater than U.S.-Russia trade, and for the other EU states listed below it was greater on average by 62 percent in that year.

If there is one factor that most influences Europe's position on sanctions, it is energy. As Table 4.2 shows, many European countries rely heavily on natural gas imports from Russia—about 15 percent is delivered through pipelines that traverse Ukraine— whereas the United States does not. In 2012, 93 percent of U.S. natural gas imports (2,980,214 million cubic feet) came from Canada, the rest from Mexico, and Russia was not among the suppliers of liquefied natural gas (LNG).[36] Of the EU countries that most rely on Russia, six (Bulgaria, Estonia, Finland, Latvia, Lithuania, and the Czech Republic) depend on it for 80 to 100 percent of their consumption, and eight (Slovakia, Slovenia, Greece, Poland, Austria, Hungary, Belgium, and Germany) for between 40 and 63 percent.

The EU can certainly reduce its dependence on Russia by increasing energy efficiency, relying more on non-hydrocarbon fuels and on LNG imports, and banking on the shale revolution to yield alternative sources of supply. But these benefits will take time to appear and will not diminish the significance of gas imports from Russia for Europe in the near term. The shale revolution has turned

the United States into the world's biggest natural gas producer—
Russia is second—but the billions of dollars that companies must
invest in terminals and other infrastructure and the complexities
of gaining certifications from the federal government mean that
exports to the EU are unlikely before 2017 or even 2018, if then.
Then there are the costs of sea-borne transportation and (energy-
intensive) liquefaction—from natural gas to LNG and back to natural gas—which would make the price unattractive, the more so
for cash-strapped Ukraine. As for non-U.S. LNG suppliers, they are
attracted by the high prices paid in Asia and would have little reason to divert sales to Europe.[37] Once American LNG exporters get
into the game, they too will eye the Asian market. Perhaps the biggest consequence of the shale revolution and the increased use of
LNG will be to reduce the price of gas. That could hurt the Russian

Gas Imports from Russia as a Percentage of Total Gas Consumption			
Country	Percentage	Country	Percentage
Armenia	100	Poland	54
Belarus	100	Austria	52
Bulgaria	100	Hungary	49
Estonia	100	Belgium	43
Finland	100	Germany	40
Lithuania	100	Serbia	40
Czech Rupublic	80	Macedonia	33
Bosnia-Herzegovina	73	Luxembourg	27
Ukraine	72	Romania	24
Slovakia	63	Italy	19
Turkey	62	France	17
Slovenia	57	United Kingdom	15
Greece	54	Netherlands	6

Table 4.2
EU gas imports from Russia. Source: Gazprom Export Figures 2013, European Commission, EU Energy in Figures Statistical Pocketbook 2013; Euro-
gas, Statistical Report 2013, http://www.eurogas.org/uploads/media/
Eurogas_Statistical_Report_2013.pdf; Margarita M Balmaceda, *The Politics of
Energy Dependency; Ukraine, Belarus, and Lithuania Between Domestic Oligarchs and Russian Pressure* (Toronto: University of Toronto Press, 2013).

economy: in 2013, taxes and export fees levied on energy and other extractive industries provided half of Russia's budget revenues, and natural gas exports netted $73 billion (and crude oil another $174 billion), or 15 percent of total export income.[38]

The upshot is that Washington's demands for toughness from the EU resembled two friends dining at an expensive restaurant, with one insisting on the sole right to choose the dishes yet refusing to pay any more than a small fraction of the bill.

The deliberations on sanctions made for discord within the EU as well. Once the United States imposed penalties on Russia, pressure began to mount on Europe to act. But European governments disagreed on which of them should do what. Each favored steps that entailed the least cost for its own economy and advocated those that transferred the cost to others. Thus France came under pressure to cut military exports to Russia, including canceling the already-signed $1.6 billion contract (which created some 1,000 jobs) for selling Mistral-class helicopter-carrying amphibious assault ships to the Russian navy. Together with the Obama administration, Britain was among the EU states calling on France to cancel the sale, and Lithuania's president even likened it to the appeasement of Nazi Germany.[39] But because arms sales to Russia help support France's military industries, the French refused to block the sale of the first of the two ships under contract and were non-committal on the second. French leaders accused Britain of hypocrisy and proposed that Britain cut Russian moguls off from London's financial and housing markets, both of which attract billions of dollars in Russian money, some of it of dubious provenance. Given its substantial trade volume with Russia, Germany was wary of sanctions generally and, like other EU states that depend heavily on Russian gas, particularly those aimed at Russia's energy sector.

The Catalyst

Despite its economic dependence on Russia, the EU had no choice but to expand sanctions on Russia after MH-17 was shot down. These new sanctions went beyond asset freezes and travel bans against additional members of the Russian economic and political elite. As the United States had already done, Europe now targeted key sectors of Russia's economy, such as banking and energy, and banned new arms deals and limited technology transfers.[40] (Washington then announced additional punitive measures of its own.) In September, because of continuing pressure from France's allies, but even more so because of Russia's escalation of the war in Ukraine, Hollande announced that the delivery of the Mistral ships would be suspended.[41] In addition, the EU extended the sanctions on Russia to capital markets and defense and "dual use" technology.[42] Moreover, the steps taken in July—asset freezes and visa bans affecting 87 individuals and entities—were expanded to additional individuals and organizations, and new agreements between the European Investment Bank and Russia and the European Bank for Reconstruction and Development were suspended.[43]

The divisions between Europe and the United States and within the EU may well have persisted, to Russia's advantage, had not MH-17 been shot out of the sky that month. That tragedy, and the difficulties encountered in retrieving passengers' remains and investigating the wreckage, transformed the sanctions debate, not only because most passengers killed were nationals of the Netherlands, an EU member. It became untenable for Europe to hold back on sanctions, both because of public outrage and because there was no letup in Moscow's support for the Donbas insurgents. Ironically, what changed the EU's position was not so much American goading but an accident traceable to a Russian-made armament. That was something Vladimir Putin could not have anticipated and certainly did not desire. What he did have control over was Russia's military intervention in Ukraine, but he chose to expand it, showing that he was prepared to absorb additional Western economic penalties for the sake of strategic gains.

If the message that the United States and the EU intended to send Moscow by ratcheting up sanctions was that Russia would pay a high price for continuing to support the Donbas insurgents, it was not received. The Kremlin's initial reaction to the added sanctions was to shrug them off and to state that it would not be provoked into knee-jerk retaliation. But Putin evidently directed his economic team to explore the range of feasible responses, the concomitant costs to Russia, and the likely effect on Western economies. In the first week of August, having already blocked the sales of Polish fruits and vegetables and various Ukrainian food products, Moscow unveiled its own sanctions on the United States and the EU, banning meat, fish, produce, and dairy sales in Russia for one year by countries that had applied sanctions on it. The losses are again asymmetrical: the EU shipped $16.5 billion worth of these items in 2013, not a trivial sum, even though it accounted for less than 7 percent of all EU food exports (though a larger share of individual countries). For the United States, by contrast, food sales to Russia amounted to $1.6 billion in that same year, or less than 1 percent of its total income from such exports.[44]

Moscow announced that other measures were under consideration, including prohibitions on the use of Siberian airspace by Western airlines bound for Asia (a move that, if applied, was expected to affect 14 EU carriers) and on the importation of automobiles, aircraft, and warships from countries that had placed economic restrictions on Russia. In addition, Ukrainian aircraft were banned from using Russian airspace for certain destinations. That added to the pressures already placed on Kyiv by Moscow. These included demands for repayment of nearly $4 billion in arrears owed to Gazprom, cuts in Russia natural gas sales, and demands for high prices ($385 per thousand cubic feet, a 34 percent increase from the pre-crisis price), and prepayment in the future.[45] Ukraine arranged to cover half of its gas needs (about 30 billion cubic meters) by "reverse flow" purchases from Poland, Hungary, and Slovakia, but that still left a substantial deficit as winter approached.[46] To show that re-exporting Russian gas to Ukraine would bring pain, the Kremlin cut gas exports to Poland by about 24 percent in September and to Slovakia by 50 percent the following month. Hungary got the message and stopped reselling Russian gas to Ukraine within days of a meeting at the end of September between its prime minister, Viktor Orban, and the head of Gazprom, Alexei Miller.[47]

Russia's response to Western sanctions was intended to show both that it would not yield to public pressure and that two could play the sanctions game. The EU dismissed Moscow's moves as political—an adjective Russia had earlier applied to Western sanctions—and vowed not to be rattled, which was precisely Moscow's line about the West's economic pressure. Theatrics aside, the true costs—economic and political—to both sides could not be predicted with any confidence at so early a stage.

The sanctions prohibiting loans and technology sales to Russian companies will undoubtedly hurt the Russian economy. The costs to Russia are likely to include higher inflation, a further slowdown in economic growth (the growth rate for 2014 was expected to be a mere at 0.5 percent), and higher interest rates resulting from the effort to slow the quickening pace of capital flight, which the European Central Bank estimated at $220 billion for the first half of 2014, in contrast to the Russian Central Bank's figure of $74 billion.[48]

On the other hand, Russia has comparatively little external debt ($716 billion as of March 2014), and this figure is also low relative to GDP: 33 percent, substantially below the figures for the United States and Europe. Likewise, Russia's public debt relative to GDP (7.9 percent) is among the lowest in the world.[49] Moreover, Russia's large financial reserves ($478 billion, the world's fifth largest) will enable its central bank to lend to companies affected by Western banking restrictions and to cushion the blow. Though heavily reliant on food imports from the EU, Russia can fill some of the gap by turning to New Zealand, Brazil, China, and Turkey, among other suppliers—and has done so. There are bound to be side effects in the form of higher prices, shortages, and diminishing currency reserves, but the Russian leadership seemed to have taken account of these and concluded that they were worth the price, that it would not face revolts at home, and that it can cope by turning to alternative food suppliers in Latin America, Turkey, and China.

In short, by mid-2014, Europe and Russia had settled on an identical strategy: using economic pressure to change the other's behavior. Yet neither had any reliable way to predict how painful the punishment would prove to the other side, how much pain it is prepared to endure, and how much weight it attaches to economic gains and losses relative to pride, resolve, reputation, and other intangibles.[50] Ultimately, no one could answer the central question a priori. Was Russia more vulnerable because the sanctions had hit its all-important energy sector by cutting off its big oil and gas firms from Western capital and technology and because Russians are economically less well off than Europeans? Or would Russia's authoritarian polity and Putin's persisting popularity enable Moscow to withstand the pressure longer than democratic European countries facing low growth and high unemployment?

This much was clear: sanctions were not inducing the Russian leadership to change course in Ukraine. Despite the concerns voiced by some experts in Russia about their harmful long-run effects for the economy, Putin's popularity (83 percent in July 2014 and 84 percent in August) increased after sanctions were imposed, and external economic pressure appeared to have produced a rally-around-the-flag among Russians.[51] Likewise, Europe's unity held, even though two prime ministers, Robert Fico of Slovakia and Viktor Orban of Hungary, criticized the sanctions as an ill-considered move that would hurt Europe, and their Czech counterpart, Bohuslav Sobotka, opposed further ones, warning of a "drawn-out trade war."[52] What remained unclear was how long EU unity on sanctions would endure given the deepening European economic crisis and the inherent complexities of maintaining cohesion among twenty-eight countries.

NATO: The Pre-Crisis Context

During the Cold War, composing a succinct statement on NATO's raison d'être would have been easy.[53] It might have read as follows: NATO exists to deter, and if necessary defeat, a Warsaw Pact attack on Western Europe. Whether the Pact was formed to maintain Soviet control over the East European communist bloc or to conquer or "Finlandize" Western Europe was debated then, and continues to be, but this much was clear: throughout the Cold War, the quip of NATO's first Secretary-General, Lord Ismay, that the alliance was meant "to keep the Russians out, the Americans in, and the Germans down" was widely, even if implicitly, accepted by its members. And despite intermittent discord within NATO, most Europeans believed that it worked, and was important to them, in each of these three respects.

Once the Soviet Union dissolved, NATO's rationale was no longer self-evident, and Ismay-like formulations were nowhere to be found.[54] The alliance was of course determined to demonstrate its continuing relevance, and one way in which it did so, starting in1996, was by expanding eastward.

But NATO's enlargement created two problems. First, it made Russia suspicious and resentful, especially once it became apparent that the project for a larger NATO did not encompass Russia, beyond the anodyne Permanent Joint Council created in 1997 and the NATO-Russia Council, its 2002 successor. The alliance's expansion incited a backlash in Russia, particularly from nationalists and communists, but not just from them. Yet there was no such resistance at the official level as soon as discussions over NATO's expansion began; Moscow's reaction in the initial years of Yeltsin's presidency was benign, especially since the discussions then included a partnership between the alliance and Russia, and even Russian membership.

But the mood in Russia was shifting by the mid-1990s, and Yeltsin's replacement of his first foreign minister, Andrei Kozyrev, with Evgenii Primakov in 1996 was a bellwether. Opinion polls and statements by influential Russians representing diverse political orientation showed deep concern that an alliance that symbolized the Cold War was advancing toward Russia's borders—and at a time when the country was experiencing an economic and military collapse and Western governments were declaring the end of the east-west ideological and military rivalry and proffering plans for partnership.[55] This perplexity and resentment, which Putin would later tap and mobilize to develop his brand of red-blooded nationalism, was discounted, even dismissed, by Western proponents of expansion, who at best seemed puzzled by Russian anxieties given what they took to be the purity of NATO's motives.[56] Lacking was any inclination on their part to imagine what the American reaction would have been had the Soviet Union won the Cold War, incorporated Canada and Mexico and the other Central American states into the Warsaw Pact, and declared that Washington had no cause to worry, its historic vital interest in these places notwithstanding.

It is true that NATO expansion resulted at least as much from the desire of states who were part of the USSR or the "Soviet bloc" (to use a Cold War archaism) to become members as from a campaign driven by Washington. But that distinction was lost on Russian leaders: for them what mattered was the expansion itself, which occurred amidst professions of friendship for Russia and toasts to the end of Cold War–era enmity. Moreover, the discussions about inviting Czech Republic, Hungary, and Poland to join NATO—which began in the early 1990s and led to a formal invitation in July 1997 and their official admission in March 1999—coincided roughly with NATO's military operations in the Balkans. In Moscow's eyes, the alliance's expansion and its intervention in places that had long been strategically of great importance to Russia were related.[57]

Likewise, contrary to an oft-repeated claim, Mikhail Gorbachev was not given a formal commitment that NATO would not expand eastward as a quid pro quo for his acceptance of a unified Germany within NATO. When the Soviet Union was unraveling, no one envisioned, let alone planned, NATO expansion as it would later occur.[58] The assurance to Gorbachev in the Soviet Union's twilight years pertained to the stationing of NATO troops in the former German Democratic Republic (East Germany). But whether a promise was made about expansion is beside the point. It is hard to imagine a Russian leader who would have been phlegmatic about NATO's extension into states that once were part of the USSR or the Warsaw Pact, even if a no-expansion pledge was never given.

Second, enlargement made it harder to create consensus on the alliance's purpose, not least because it occurred so rapidly and under circumstances utterly different from the Cold War, when the Warsaw Pact's existence concentrated European minds. At its inception in 1949, NATO had 12 members. Only four additional states were admitted to its ranks during the following four decades. But between 1999 and 2009, membership nearly doubled to its current twenty-eight.[59] The consequences for cohesion were evident well before then. In the lead-up to the Iraq war, New Europe (as Donald Rumsfeld famously called the inhabitants of the continent's East) backed the Bush administration; Old Europe (his label for NATO's established members in Western Europe) was divided, and some of its governments, France in particular, broke publicly with Washington. The same division was apparent on the issue of whether Russia was a foe or a potential partner; given their location and history, NATO's newest members, from East-Central Europe, were far leerier about Russia than its European old guard. To complicate matters, NATO's expansion coincided with discussions about extending its mission beyond Europe and embracing "out-of-area" operations, i.e., missions that transcended obligations under the alliance's treaty. This had always been a sensitive issue within the alliance (Europe understandably preferred a continental focus), but it became more contentious once NATO actually started intervening in extra-European conflicts on the theory that, as Senator Richard Lugar observed in 1993, the alliance had to either "go out of area or out of business."[60]

One controversy—evident during the missions in Bosnia, Kosovo, Afghanistan, Iraq, and Libya, all out-of-area in that they extended beyond NATO's borders and were not responses to an attack on a member—concerned burden sharing. Every NATO state besides the United States carried a lighter load during the Cold War thanks to Washington's security guarantee, which was enabled by America's massive economic and military superiority. There were, of course, variations within NATO on the percentage of GDP devoted to defense spending, but the European allies mostly devoted a much smaller proportion than did the United States. This imbalance didn't matter much so long as the Cold War raged, but in a post-Soviet world, Washington's tolerance waned, and Europe, which had long since become an economic competitor, was called on to spend more on defense.

The exhortations were occasioned in particular by the evident disparities in Europe's ability to project power and sustain missions far afield. Despite calls for greater fairness in contributing to the alliance, it still appeared to be largely an American operation, with able assists from a few members, principally France and the UK. The air campaign in Bosnia and Kosovo made this clear as early as the 1990s, and even the 2011 Libya operation, in which some NATO states played a prominent part, revealed most European NATO members' inability to sustain distant missions, even against a third-rate opponent, without essential American support, including aerial refueling, cruise missiles, and electronic countermeasures.[61] Burden sharing was not, however, just about budgets; it was also about fighting, and there was a contrast between America and most of its Atlantic allies when it came to willingness to wage war in non-European conflicts. This was particularly evident in the Iraq and Afghanistan wars, during which American forces and a few allies, some of whom did not belong to NATO, did the heavy lifting.[62]

The expansion of NATO's membership and mission did not for these reasons turn out to be quite the tonic that its advocates hoped it would be. It was against this background that NATO faced the 2014 Ukraine conflict.

NATO Relevance: No More Doubts?

The crisis was very much "in area": several NATO countries, above all Poland and the Baltic states, were unnerved by Russia's absorption of Crimea and its support for separatists in the Donbas, which appeared to foreshadow an irredentist move there as well. It did not take long for pundits to proclaim that the confrontation over Ukraine had conclusively established that NATO remained relevant, no matter the end of the Cold War, and would emerge strengthened from the latest test. This was certainly the theme struck from the onset by the outgoing Secretary General Anders Fogh Rasmussen, in the alliance's official statements and in speeches made by the leaders of NATO states.[63]

Yet the belief that the Ukraine crisis will solidify NATO may rest on false hopes.

First, the problems that expansion has created for consensus among the allies will persist and even manifest themselves in Russia-related matters. Once the dust kicked up by the Ukraine crisis settles, the differences on how to deal with Russia will reemerge. The NATO states nearest to the Russia will, owing to anxieties produced by propinquity and memories of having been dominated or ruled by Imperial Russia or the Soviet Union, seek firm commitments from their other European allies, especially the most powerful ones: Britain, France, and Germany. But the latter are likely, because of their distance from Russia and their more robust military capabilities, to feel less vulnerable. Moreover, the EU's big three have substantial commercial and political ties with Russia. There will thus be an imbalance between the anxieties of NATO's eastern wing and the willingness of the alliance's European powerhouses to allay them. For the former, Russia will be a perennial problem, even a threat; for the latter it will be a potential partner with whom there are good years and bad ones but always common interests that need to be protected, with the long run in mind.

Second, rather than energizing NATO to resume its expansion, Putin's conduct in Ukraine will likely make the alliance's most powerful states—those that would assume the biggest risks in the event of a war—reluctant to extend protection to additional states on Russia's doorstep. These prospective allies are all too weak to deter Russia and have a history of conflict with it, and this increases the odds that they might one day redeem the pledge of protection provided by Article V of the April 1949 North Atlantic Treaty.[64] For this reason, most members of Old NATO were relieved that Georgia was not part of the pact during its 2008 war with Russia; and an equal number were likely thankful in 2014 that Ukraine was not, for the same reason. In the United States, President Obama was not alone in consistently ruling out, from the start of the crisis, war with Russia over Ukraine.[65] Influential hardline critics of Russia, such Senator John McCain, did as well.[66] So did the leaders of the European states; indeed all were relieved by the American reaction, even, or perhaps particularly, those geographically closest to

Russia. As for Americans generally, polls showed that they were overwhelmingly opposed to using force in defense of Ukraine and that a majority even rejected deeper involvement. Though the surveys showed that the crisis had increased Americans' mistrust of Moscow, only a small majority opined that Russia was a serious threat.[67] The results were similar even after the downing of MH-17: most Americans were against increased involvement generally, and a big majority opposed using military means, including airstrikes, or even arming Ukraine.[68]

Amidst doubts about its capacity to defend Poland and the Baltic states, as well as calls from leaders there for the long-term deployment of combat troops in their countries—Poland asked for 10,000—NATO sought to reassure its nervous eastern members, regardless of Russia's reaction. The alliance called on Russia to pull back the troops it had massed on Ukraine's borders, to end its aid to the Donbas separatists, and to withdraw its soldiers from Ukraine. But there was no consensus within the alliance on placing substantial numbers of troops in Poland and the Baltics. Key NATO states, such as Germany, made it clear that they were opposed to such action (even though they would support less dramatic steps, such as more frequent exercises), to the evident frustration of the Balts and the Poles.[69] "There is no appetite in the West," a *Time* report noted, "for military action to preserve Ukraine's sovereignty, despite a 1994 pact [i.e., the Budapest Memorandums discussed in Chapter 1] among Russia, Britain and the U.S. pledging to honor its borders."[70] As the influential German magazine *Der Spiegel* observed about NATO's closed-door planning about increasing the capacity to defend its eastern allies:

> [T]he German government dreads a discussion of new
> Western military plans. Both the chancellor and the

foreign minister prefer a more cautious approach to diplomacy in the conflict with Russia. Officials in Berlin say that actions that Russia could interpret as the West flexing its muscle would lead "directly to disaster." In addition, German public opinion is extremely opposed to upgrading NATO under the premise that the West must arm itself for a military conflict with Russia. Chancellor Angela Merkel is unwilling to consider an increase in defense spending, and she is certainly not interested in setting off an uncontrollable German debate over the notion of German soldiers potentially risking their lives for the Baltic countries.[71]

Still, by August evidence mounted that Russia was scaling up its arms supplies to the alliance, that an increasing number of Russians were volunteering (many of them former members of the military or active duty soldiers on leave), and that Russian military units were directly participating in the conflict. NATO faced the challenge of maintaining its unity by doing enough to reassure the Balts and Poles but without establishing a large, permanent presence in its eastern flank, a move that was unpalatable to the alliance's heavyweights (Germany, France, Italy, and Spain among them). Another contentious issue was supplying arms and training to Ukraine's army. On this too the divisions within NATO were similar, with Germany taking an early position against it on the grounds that it would aggravate the war, and the alliance's eastern members, among them Lithuania, Poland, and Romania, explicitly supporting it.[72] (Latvia and Estonia, each of which has an ethnic Russian population that accounts for more than 25 percent of the total, remained circumspect on this point.)

Not surprisingly, the alliance's willingness to help Ukraine in tangible ways was limited to providing instant meals

("meals-ready-to-eat") and "non-lethal" equipment. European leaders understood that NATO would have had to contemplate war with Russia had Ukraine been an ally and come under attack. Despite her opposition to putting troops in Poland and the Baltics, Merkel knew that the failure to defend these states in the event that they were attacked would have torn the alliance apart, and the German chancellor and her fellow European leaders doubtless realized that this would apply equally to commitments extended to Ukraine were it to join NATO. Thus the 2014 crisis will likely decrease the chances of NATO membership for Ukraine, Georgia, and Moldova. They may eventually receive Membership Action Plans, but that could prove a sop amounting to an indefinite wait in the antechamber.

Third, the fracas over Ukraine will not be the godsend that buries NATO's burden sharing dispute. The disparity between the contributions of the United States and its allies remains glaring. The U.S. defense budget will necessarily dwarf that of individual NATO countries, and even their combined expenditures: the United States is a superpower with worldwide military commitments. But the size of defense budgets is not the relevant measure. What counts, and will continue to do so, is the relative effort of NATO states and the steps they take (or fail to take) to increase the military capabilities relevant to the security of the alliance.

Nearly seven decades have passed since World War II ended and Europe lay shattered. During that time Europe recovered and once again became a center of global economic power. By 2010, the EU accounted for 26 percent of global GDP, the United States for 23 percent. As a consequence, Europe and the United States have long been fierce competitors in the global marketplace.[73] Yet the disparity in burden sharing lingers. This is clear from a comparison of the relative proportions of their GDP that alliance members allocate to defense.[74] The average for European NATO members in 2013 was 1.6 percent, while for the United States it was 4.3 percent. This was not a one-off discrepancy. The data on sequential four-year averages since 1990 show a near-steady decline in contributions from European NATO members. The highpoint was 1990–94, 2.7 percent, but the average had dropped to 1.7 by 2010 and to 1.6 in 2011, where it has remained since. By contrast, the average for the United States between 2009 and 2013 was 4.9. Between 2009 and 2013, only three European NATO states (France, Greece, and the UK) devoted 2 percent or more; eight were at or above 1.5, and thirteen were below 1.3.

GDP-defense ratio comparisons have their limits. But the picture doesn't change when it comes to operational efforts. These include

NATO Defense Spending as a Percentage of GDP			
Years	NATO Europe	United States	NATO Total
1990-1994*	2.5	4.5	3.4
1995-1999*	2.1	3.2	2.6
2000-2004*	1.9	3.3	2.6
2005-2009*	1.8	4.4	2.9
2009	1.7	5.3	3.3
2010	1.7	5.3	3.3
2011	1.6	4.8	3
2012	1.6	4.5	2.9
2013	1.6	4.4	2.9
*average			

Table 4.3
NATO defense spending comes disproportionately from the United States. Years marked with an asterisk report average spending. Source: NATO, Public Diplomacy Division, "Financial and Economic Data Relating to NATO Defense," February 24, 2014, http://www.nato.int/nato_static/assets/pdf/pdf_topics/20140224_140224-PR2014-028-Defence-exp.pdf.

coordinated, Europe-wide efforts to improve efficiency in procurement, increase "power projection" capabilities (air-and sea-lift), devise an effective division of military responsibilities that avoids duplication and cashes in on comparative advantage, improve inter-operability, and narrow the U.S.-Europe military technology gap.[75] The prospects that much will happen on these fronts are slim for several reasons. Political support in Europe for boosting defense spending is weak at best generally, and the post-2008 economic crisis has made it even weaker. As the continent's population continues to age (and at a faster rate than in the United States), the claims of the elderly and infirm on the welfare state will increase, reducing further whatever enthusiasm does exist for boosting military strength. Europe is struggling to trim expenditures on public services. The tradition of extensive state-supplied social services and benefits (and public expectations related to them) and the power of unions have been, and will remain, far stronger than in the United States. The prospect that cuts in spending on social services will be used to beef up defense budgets is therefore remote, all the more so given Europe's post-2008 economic plight.

During the Cold War, the burden sharing controversy was muted. During the first two decades after World War II, Europe was recovering, the United States thriving. But in the twenty-first century, polls show that Americans are apprehensive about their job prospects, income inequality, reduced social mobility, the caliber of schools and infrastructure, and the quality of life in store for their children. While some polls show that a majority does not favor cutting defense spending, others show that it supports capping, even cutting, the resources that flow to the Pentagon.[76] But Americans are likely to agree that their wealthy allies should do more to protect themselves, and that sentiment will shape attitudes in the Congress and the executive branch.[77]

The Ukraine crisis will therefore not diminish the burden sharing debate within the alliance and may indeed amplify it at a time when Europe's economic problems make it even more reluctant to spend more on arms. But if NATO does in fact expand further eastward, Washington will push its partners harder to spend more to meet the new obligations—and be less forgiving of their traditional reluctance to oblige.

It is thus unlikely that the Ukraine crisis will provide a fillip to NATO and an opportunity to articulate a new purpose. There is no doubt that the crisis has frayed Russia's relationship with the West badly and that repairing the damage will prove hard and protracted. But because of Russia's economic, political, and military significance, NATO's most influential European members will eventually extend the olive branch to Moscow, the European firms that trade with and invest in Russia urging them on. For its part, Russia will have many reasons, both economic and strategic, to reciprocate. It does not want to be a pariah that is deprived of the economic benefits of trade with the West and placed in diplomatic isolation. Nor does it wish to burn bridges with the West and to be left dependent on China, a rising power and country with which, the current China-Russia "strategic partnership" notwithstanding, Russia has had a troubled history and a 2,670-mile land border.

The contention that the Ukraine crisis has kindled something akin to a new Cold War and has solidified NATO is misplaced. While it was indubitably an important moment for NATO, it will not prove to be a defining one.

5 Ukraine's Prospects

The outlook for Ukraine is highly challenging even in the best-case scenario. Both its domestic circumstances and its international position have been badly damaged and will push to the limit the abilities of even the most capable and committed leadership to manage them.

Possible Scenarios

At the time of this writing, the outcome of the crisis cannot be foretold. However, we can say with certainty that the crisis will be long-term, spanning a period of months and probably years. Schematically, the future course of the crisis can be presented in terms of three possible scenarios:

A FROZEN CONFLICT. The conflict in eastern Ukraine becomes a standoff with low-grade fighting continuing indefinitely but with the September 2014 ceasefire and the accompanying agreements at least nominally observed by all sides. Russia in effect establishes a protectorate in eastern Ukraine similar to Transnistria, and the region morphs into a long-term frozen conflict with no solution in sight.

RUSSIA INVADES. The September ceasefire breaks down and the conflict in eastern Ukraine escalates again and leads to a direct Russian military intervention beyond the Donetsk and Luhansk regions; Russia mounts a full-scale military invasion of Ukraine and occupies major parts of it along the left bank of the river Dnipro, possibly including Kyiv, leaving a truncated independent Ukrainian state that includes parts of central and western regions of the country.

UKRAINE WINS. Kyiv achieves complete military victory in eastern Ukraine, and the Russian separatists are defeated.

Of the three scenarios, the first appears to be the most likely. The prospect of a direct Russian military invasion of Ukraine cannot be dismissed. However, throughout the crisis, the Kremlin has demonstrated repeatedly its reluctance to mount a full-scale invasion of Ukraine and, along with it, bear the burden of military occupation and the associated political, economic, and military fallout.

The frozen conflict scenario also appears to be the most desirable outcome for the Kremlin because it would spare it the costs and the uncertainties of a military occupation of eastern Ukraine, while presenting it with a considerable source of leverage for intervening in Ukrainian domestic affairs. Crimea, as a result of annexation by Russia, can no longer play the role of Moscow's instrument for intervening in Ukrainian domestic affairs.

The second scenario—Russia invades—appears to be less likely because of the economic and political costs it entails for Russia. Having declared his commitment to intervene on behalf of co-ethnics, Vladimir Putin did not intervene in May of 2014 after a tragic fire in Odessa took the lives of more than forty Russian sympathizers. Putin avoided the added commitment of supporting the Luhansk and Donetsk referendums that proclaimed their status as independent republics. Had he not disassociated himself from their declarations of independence, the pressure to intervene militarily would have been much greater. Even when the Ukrainian military was gaining and the separatists were in retreat, Putin resisted the calls—from eastern Ukraine, as well as from inside Russia—to intervene directly. Instead, he chose to send in Russian military personnel and equipment covertly, denying direct Russian involvement, and did not send the Russian army to occupy territories beyond those held by the separatists in the Donetsk and Luhansk regions. While the threat of a direct military intervention by Russian Armed Forces cannot be ruled out, it appears to be the Kremlin's choice of last resort.

The third scenario—Ukraine wins—appears to be highly unlikely, despite the temporary advances made by the Ukrainian forces on the battlefield during the summer campaign of 2014. Their progress was uneven, and the separatists, even when in retreat, were able to inflict significant casualties on Kyiv's units. Russian active support for the separatists when they were retreating and appeared on the verge of being defeated has demonstrated Moscow's commitment to support the separatists. The Kremlin has signaled repeatedly that while it is highly reluctant to intervene in eastern Ukraine directly, it is not prepared to allow Kyiv to achieve a total victory on the battlefield over the separatists—and thus over Russia.

No matter which of these scenarios comes to pass, Ukraine will face immense challenges. These will cover the full spectrum of domestic politics, economic development, national security, and foreign policy.

Domestic Politics

The February revolution in Kyiv was only a first step toward the development of a new political order in Ukraine. The separatist conflict that followed, which Russia has actively supported, has resulted in a significant regional split within the Ukrainian polity. The split was undoubtedly aggravated and probably instigated in large measure by Russian interference in Ukrainian domestic politics and by a massive propaganda campaign designed to discredit the new Kyiv government and stoke fears of a western-Ukrainian domination of the political order. Although in large part artificially created, the split has become a political reality, which is likely to get worse as the crisis progresses and takes an increasing human toll. It will not heal in the present circumstances of an active military conflict in eastern Ukraine and the Kyiv government's pursuit of a military victory over the separatists.

The May 2014 presidential election, while conferring legitimacy on the government in Kyiv, which until then had been only a provisional body, had its limitations. Because of the fighting in eastern Ukraine, many of the region's potential voters were unable to cast their ballots. The election was indeed national in scope, but the ongoing military conflict carries with it inherent limitations for voter participation.

The same limitations apply to the other critical legitimizing step—the October 2014 parliamentary election. The unstable situation in eastern Ukraine has been highly disruptive to everyday life in the region, to say nothing of its impact on the conduct of a fair and free election open to all potential voters.

The stress of war and the parliamentary election have revealed growing fissures in the coalition that spearheaded the revolution and propelled Petro Poroshenko to the presidency. Prime Minister Arseniy Yatsenyuk grew critical of the president for the terms of the truce with Russia and the separatists he accepted in September 2014.[1] Poroshenko's key challenge in the new Rada will be to build a solid governing coalition—a task with which virtually all his predecessors had to struggle.

With presidential and parliamentary elections encumbered by these limitations, the legitimacy of the government in Kyiv is bound to remain challenged in parts of eastern Ukraine, and this will stand in the way of national reconciliation. The Kyiv government's other actions, such as the lustration law passed in October, are likely to make reconciliation more challenging.[2]

Beyond bridging the political divide, the Ukrainian leadership will face the additional difficulty of consolidating its power and authority, which are likely to continue to be challenged by the country's powerful class of business tycoons. The war has given rise to private armies, raised and financed by—and answerable to—the oligarchs. These armies or militias have reportedly been carrying much of the burden of fighting in the East.[3] The active role of the oligarchs in the conduct of the war in the East and their sponsorship of militias are likely to make them even more powerful and the Kyiv authorities even more dependent on them than they were before the start of the conflict. It is unlikely that the militias simply will submit to Kyiv's will, especially if the government's legitimacy is compromised and its policies impinge on their business interests.

In addition to the oligarchs, the Ukrainian authorities will also have to contend with some of the most radical nationalist elements, who are likely to oppose any move by the government to seek reconciliation and compromise with the East. The departure of some of the most prominent Maidan activists from the government could pose a serious challenge to the Poroshenko administration at a time when it is still consolidating power and building a national consensus in support of its reform agenda.[4] The resignation of nationalist leader Andriy Parubiy (head of the Defense and National Security Council) and prominent anti-corruption crusader Tetyana Chornovyl (head of the newly established anti-corruption agency) in frustration over the government's lack of progress on the war front or in the fight against corruption point to a potential challenge to the Poroshenko administration from its own camp.

By far the biggest challenge facing the Kyiv government is the state of the economy. The economy is estimated to contract in 2014 and 2015 by over 7 and 4 percent, respectively, according to the IMF.[5] But this projection is likely not the final word, and the economy's condition could grow even worse. The initial $17 billion aid package from the IMF to Ukraine provided in April 2014 has been widely seen as insufficient.[6] As early as February 2014, the government of Ukraine stated that it would need $35 billion more to meet its obligations in 2014 and 2015.[7] In September 2014, the IMF effectively confirmed that estimate when it projected that Ukraine would need $19 billion more in additional financing before the end of 2015.[8] Ukraine's ability to handle this debt burden is also in question and it could become an additional impediment to future growth.

IMF assistance to Ukraine is conditioned on Ukraine's ability to implement a series of far-reaching reforms, including some that are bound to be extremely unpopular and painful for the general public, such as cuts to the government's social spending programs and energy subsidies. Early reform efforts have run into opposition from the Yanukovych-era parliament, as have previous attempts to introduce reforms throughout the history of independent Ukraine. The new parliament, when faced with popular disaffection over belt-tightening, is also likely to act as a brake on the government's reform agenda.

Moreover, many of the structural reforms are bound to have a disproportionate effect in the country's eastern provinces, where most of the Soviet industrial inheritance is concentrated. While some of these enterprises have benefited from an infusion of funds by their oligarch owners, most are legacy Soviet enterprises that have survived thanks to heavy state subsidies and cheap Russian energy. Absent these, two vital sources of livelihood for eastern Ukraine will not be able to survive, adding to the social and political pressure and perception that Kyiv's painful reforms are targeted disproportionately, and punitively, at the East. These reforms are also likely to affect the interests of many Ukrainian oligarchs with empires located in eastern Ukraine, who have benefited from state support and sweetheart deals with Russia. The lack of a political reconciliation process in the East will make these inherently difficult reforms harder still.

The International Context

The domestic challenges facing Ukraine are closely tied to the no less difficult international environment it is certain to face in coming months and years. Chief among them are Ukraine's disrupted and profoundly transformed relationship with Russia, on the one hand, and its uncertain relationship with Europe and the United States, on the other.

The question of Ukraine's relationship with NATO has been one of the most neuralgic issues for Moscow and probably one of the most important drivers of Russian actions. As mentioned in Chapters 2 and 3, at its 2008 summit in Bucharest, the alliance pledged to admit Ukraine someday. Yet Ukrainian attitudes toward membership in the alliance have fluctuated over time. In 2010, 51 percent of Ukrainians had an unfavorable view of NATO and opposed membership in the alliance, while 28 percent favored joining it.[9] Over a period of five years, the proportion of Ukrainians who saw NATO as a source of protection for their country changed only slightly from 15 percent in 2008 to 17 percent in 2013.[10] In May 2014—well into the crisis with Russia—42 percent still opposed joining the alliance, while 36 percent favored it.[11]

As these numbers indicate, the crisis has pushed many Ukrainians toward a more favorable view of NATO. However, these figures suggest that even in the midst of a crisis with Russia, and with Ukrainian sovereignty and independence at stake, support for NATO membership in Ukraine is far from overwhelming, and, in the event it becomes once again an active policy choice, it will almost certainly be divisive among Ukrainians.

Furthermore, throughout the crisis NATO leaders have shown no interest in offering Ukraine membership in the alliance. While condemning Russia's annexation of Crimea and its continuing military interference in eastern Ukraine, NATO leaders have made clear that a military conflict with Russia over Ukraine is out of the question. This stance was reaffirmed during NATO's summit in Wales in September 2014. As noted earlier, in chapter 3, the crisis is likely to diminish further NATO's appetite for extending its defensive umbrella over Ukraine. This crisis has demonstrated the risk the alliance would have faced had it invited Ukraine into its ranks as a result of the pledge made at the Bucharest summit in 2008. Even Ukraine's most fervent champions within NATO are not ready to risk war with Russia in order to demonstrate their loyalty to Kyiv.

The crisis has also presented Ukraine with a host of economic problems beyond those it already faced. Prior to the conflict, Russia accounted for 25 percent, or $16 billion, of Ukraine's exports. Russia has already imposed a number of trade sanctions on Ukraine in retribution for its signing an AA and DCFTA with the EU and has threatened more sanctions in the future. Eventually, the signing of the DCFTA promises to bring about significant benefits stemming from improved access to the EU market. But many of these benefits are conditioned on Ukraine's ability to enact and implement a large number of EU trade regulations and quality standards. In the near term, however, it is not clear that gains from the DCFTA will make up for the losses incurred by Ukrainian businesses as a result of the loss of access to the Russian market. The fact that the free trade agreement will not be implemented until the end of 2015 holds out the possibility for Ukraine to retain access to the Russian market, but raises doubts about the future of Ukraine's access to European markets, undercuts its reform momentum, and continues its dependence on Russia.

Russia supplies nearly two-thirds of Ukraine's natural gas needs.[12] Ukraine's debt to Russia and the price of future gas deliveries remain the most contentious issues in the energy relationship between the two countries. Disagreements between them are certain to continue with Ukraine chronically struggling to meet its repayment obligations and Russia using gas as an instrument of pressuring Ukraine. In the absence of political goodwill between the two countries, the challenge of resolving future gas disputes is certain to be greater. A Russian decision to cut gas deliveries to Ukraine, threatened on many occasions (and carried out more than once), will either leave Kyiv without its key energy source or with the option of siphoning gas from Russian deliveries downstream to Europe and thus causing a crisis there.

Although the revolution in Ukraine occurred under the banner of European integration, and the crisis in Russian-Ukrainian relations was caused by the prospect of Ukraine's signing of the AA and DCFTA with the EU, membership in the EU—the ultimate goal of European integration—remains a distant prospect for the country. While the AA and DCFTA do not preclude Ukraine's membership in the EU, they do not offer a path to joining it. At best, it is a process that could take decades, as has been the case with Turkey, which signed its own AA with the EU's predecessor, the European Economic Community, in 1963.

Thus, Ukraine's relationship with Europe, its other gravitational pole (besides Russia), is highly uncertain. While Europe has rhetorically embraced the cause of Ukraine's European integration, it has been noncommittal on EU membership for Ukraine. Although the EU has promised to provide significant assistance—totaling $15 billion dollars in grants, loans, and loan guarantees over a period of several years—it is conditioned on Ukraine's ability to implement IMF-mandated reforms.[13]

Despite Europe's best intentions, its ability to sustain assistance to and interest in Ukraine should not be taken for granted. Several factors—Europe's continuing economic malaise, limited resources, numerous demands from weaker EU members, and multiple geopolitical crises, especially in the Middle East—pose the risk of Ukraine being marginalized on the continent's policy agenda. Moreover, European solidarity in support of Ukraine and in the face of renewed concerns about the threat from Russia is already showing signs of fraying. Underlying this phenomenon is the fact that Russia is far more important to Europe—economically, politically, and in terms of its security—than Ukraine.

Leaders of some of the newest EU members—Slovakia, the Czech Republic, and Hungary—have criticized EU sanctions on Russia, pointing to their adverse economic effects on Europeans.[14] Germany, France, and the United Kingdom, each for its own set of economic interests, have been reluctant to impose more sanctions on Russia. Europe's commitment to Ukraine could collide with the realities of its transformed post–Cold War economic, political, and security ties to Russia, leaving Ukraine to tackle its challenges largely on its own.

6   Conclusion

This book began with the observation that the 2014 Ukraine crisis represents the most severe disruption in East-West relations since that term fell into disuse at the end of the Cold War. For the first time since the end of Word War II, a country that had previously committed to observe the independence, sovereignty, and territorial integrity of fellow European states has annexed a portion of its neighbor's territory. Moreover, having explicitly rejected some of the fundamental principles of European security and stability it had previously accepted, Russia has embraced a foreign policy doctrine based on ideas of ethnic kinship and asserted its right to continue to violate those basic principles.

This puts at risk not only Russia's relationship with the West, but also the entire European security architecture that the United States and its allies have been pursuing since the end of the Cold War and even undermines key elements of the post–World War II political and security arrangements in Europe. The vision of Europe whole and free, at peace with itself and its neighbors, which has guided the American-European pursuit of a new security order on the continent, has met its severest, possibly fatal, test.

The crisis has also threatened to jeopardize important European and U.S. interests beyond the continent. Many elements of the transatlantic security agenda have rested on the premise of Russia's cooperation and even, in some instances, its active support, including policies on the proliferation of nuclear and other weapons of mass destruction, as well as sensitive conventional weapons and technologies, on terrorism, and on regional conflicts such as Afghanistan, North Korea, and Iran. Russian cooperation, already tenuous before the crisis on issues such as the Middle East and some aspects of Iran's nuclear program, could disappear entirely as a consequence of the deteriorating relationship between Russia and the West.

Moreover, in addition to recreating a twenty-first century version of the East-West divide, the crisis has revealed significant divisions within the Western alliance. Europe and the United States were united in their rejection and condemnation of Russian actions in Ukraine. But as the crisis wore on, it became apparent that their interests regarding Russia vary widely. During the post–Cold War period, Europe and Russia developed a far closer relationship than did the United States and Russia, one that has evolved into a mutual dependency that would take years, probably even decades, to unwind, should the Europeans decide to dismantle it. And aside from the differences between Europe and the United States, the crisis has brought to light divisions within the EU and among the European members of NATO on the particulars on responding to Russian conduct in eastern and southern Ukraine.

The crisis also highlighted the costs and challenges—unanticipated and, until recently, unimagined—of reassuring new NATO members of the alliance's commitment to their security. The alliance was expanded on the assumption that it would no longer face threats *in* Europe—that its main challenges would be *outside* of Europe, out-of-area—and that while its Article V security guarantee to new members remained in force, it would never have to be invoked.

Russian actions shattered another long-held assumption of the post–Cold War era, namely that war and the use of force had been banished if not among all states, then certainly among major European powers. The Ukraine crisis demonstrated that this comforting belief was a fallacy.

At no point during the crisis did even the greatest of pessimists warn that there was a risk of a premeditated, head-on military collision between Russia and the West. Contributing to the risk of accidental war in this crisis was the failure of the United States and Europe to anticipate Russia's moves, which at every step exceeded Western expectations of what Russia was willing to do and the risks it was prepared to take to advance its interests. As during the 2008 Russia-Georgia war, the United States and Europe did not see the crisis coming. Although the prospect of an all-out war involving Russia and the United States remains unthinkable, neither party to this conflict should ignore the danger that small incidents could inadvertently set in motion—a spiral that would in turn culminate in war that no one intended, wanted, or thought possible, as was true in Europe in August 1914.

The analogy to 1914 is appropriate. But the lessons that Europe and the United States should heed now are not limited to the *pre*-war period—that is, to the unpredictable and uncontrollable nature of political brinkmanship and military escalation, the danger of misreading an adversary's intentions and sending ill-conceived messages to him. The danger is also in failing to draw lessons from the *post*-war period. In 1918, the major powers failed in one crucial respect: they failed to devise a blueprint for Europe that would have enmeshed the vanquished nation—Germany—in a new European security network. Europe paid a horrible price for that failure in World War II but learned the lesson of the previous disaster and, after 1945, secured Germany in the web of transatlantic institutions, thus ensuring its role as the model European citizen.

However, what was done for Germany in the 1950s was not done for Russia in the 1990s after the West "won" the Cold War and the Soviet Union collapsed. Despite early misgivings about post–World War II Germany's fate in a new European security order, the part of Germany occupied by the United States, France, and Great Britain joined NATO in 1955, was fully integrated into the West, and was integral to the project of European integration. In short, its place in Europe was never in question.

That was not the case with Russia after 1991. Its place in post–Cold War Europe, whole and free, has always been tenuous. NATO membership for Russia was never seriously considered, and if it came up, it was only as a far-fetched, theoretical possibility. Devising a new security arrangement to replace *both* Cold War structures—the Warsaw Pact and NATO—was never considered either. There was never any question as to NATO's future after the Cold War: it would continue, period.

Moreover, NATO would expand. Though NATO's enlargement to the East was not intended to threaten the Kremlin's power, it was a hedge against a resurgence of bellicose Russia. If Russia failed at its post-Soviet transformation and reverted to its old expansionist self, NATO enlargement would guard Central Europe against Russian encroachment. In the words of some of the earliest and most active advocates of NATO enlargement, Russia was a "special case." Its place in Europe was a matter of grave doubt.

Russia nevertheless remains a special case due to its size, geo-strategic position, and long imperial tradition. Many Europeans believe that Russia is not a European country, is unlikely to become one, and should not be allowed into core European institutions. Indeed, at the moment not a single Atlantic alliance member is in favor of allowing Russia into either the EC or NATO, although most avoid saying so openly.[1] The possibility of EU (or then EC) membership for Russia was not on the table either.

In other words, whereas Russia's former satellites in Central Europe and the Baltics had a clear destination at the end of their post-Communist transition and a guaranteed place in Europe's security and political structures, Russia did not. It would have to prove its European identity.

The cautious approach was understandable. Russia's size, history, political culture, and military tradition, as well as its geographic position on two continents, make integrating it a daunting task. Crucially, it sees itself as an integrator, not a state that is integrated by others. The result was the two-pronged approach Europe and the United States took to Russia. One element was to hedge against Russian resurgence as an adversary; the other was to engage Russia, and encourage its transformation in the hope that it would see the benefits of the market, democracy, and integration with the West—on the West's terms.

Those who favored hedging at the expense of engagement had a better claim on having a strategy for dealing with Russia. Now, however, they have no grounds to lament that engagement with Russia has failed, as their own advocacy of hedging undercut engagement's prospects. Those who pursued a combination of the two approaches or who simply hoped that Russia would transform itself into a market democracy and integrate with the West, had no such claim.

In the words attributed to former New York mayor Rudy Giuliani and used by many others, hope is not a strategy. The United States and Europe had a strategy for Central Europe, but they did not have a strategy for Russia. Russia remained outside key European institutions; it was not enmeshed in the transatlantic political and security network as Germany was after World War II, while Russia's economic ties to Europe and the United States have become a potential vulnerability for both sides as a result of the Ukraine crisis.

The entire post–Cold War European political and security architecture was built on the foundation of two institutions— the European Union and NATO—which did not include Russia. To advance its fundamental vision of a Europe whole, free, at peace with itself and its neighbors, Europe and the United States relied on the hope that Russia would eventually embrace them on its own accord. Alas, over two decades into the post–Cold War era, this approach turned out to have been a huge gamble. It paid off in Central Europe, but not in Russia.

The Ukraine crisis is undoubtedly a pivotal event for Europe. But Ukraine is not the cause of the crisis. It is rather a symptom of an even larger problem for Europe. Europe's problem is with Russia, and its principal political, security, and economic challenges for the coming years will be to develop a new strategy for dealing with its giant neighbor. This strategy will have to be built on a realistic understanding of Russia rather than on what the West would like it to be and hopes it will one day become. It will remain a monumental task for the transatlantic community for years to come. Unless it is tackled with the ruthless realism and serious resources it deserves, stability and security in Europe will prove elusive.

Acknowledgments

I am indebted to many people who, in varying ways and from different locales, helped make this book possible.

At bucolic Kezar Lake, New Hampshire, a writer's paradise: Cathy Popkin, incomparable critic, stylist, and so much more; Lisa Lopez and Victor Del Vecchio, for animated discussions; Dick and Sandy Reilein, for inspiration.

In New York City: Lekha Menon and Zoë Menon, my peerless pair; Alex Motyl, ever gracious despite our opposing views on some issues covered in this volume; Emily Holland, exemplary research assistant; Jack Snyder; Vartan Gregorian; Tom Graham; Michael Frank and Jo Anne Schlesinger; Hugh Millard; Dan DiSalvo, for wide-ranging conversations; Bruce Cronin and Vince Boudreau for that essential requirement: time; Anne and Bernard Spitzer, for their generosity; Tom Graham, for insightful comments on parts of the manuscript; Lia Friedman, for her eagle eye.

In Washington, D.C.: Anne and Michael Mandelbaum, for always being there; Gene Rumer, coauthor extraordinaire; Jacob Heilbrunn and Harry Kazianis of *The National Interest*, for allowing me to road test some of the ideas that appear in these pages.

In Los Angeles: Cherry Gee, Nick Goldberg, and Sue Horton of the *Los Angeles Times*, where other ideas in this book first took wing; Ann Brenoff of the *Huffington Post*, for opening the door to the blogosphere.

In Boston: Deb Chasman of *Boston Review*, an exceptional editor, who proposed this book and somehow persuaded me it could be written; Matt Lord, also of *Boston Review*, for his superb editorial skills and meticulousness.

—Rajan Menon

I am grateful to Raj Menon for inviting me to join him in this project. He is a great partner whose energy and intellect have made this book possible.

My employer the Carnegie Endowment for International Peace offered me the time and the intellectual latitude to work on this book. I was fortunate to join Carnegie at the outset of the crisis in Ukraine and could not ask for a better environment to think and write about it.

Andrew Weiss has been a friend and colleague of many years who encouraged me to come to Carnegie. I am indebted to him for that and for his insights into Russia and Ukraine which helped me greatly and shaped my own ideas. Tom Graham, Jim Collins, Balazs Jarabik, and Bob Nurick influenced my thinking about this crisis and its consequences. My father Boris Rumer contributed to this project more than I can describe.

Deb Chasman and Matt Lord of *Boston Review* guided this book with skill and patience.

Special thanks go to my family for putting up with me throughout this project.

—Eugene Rumer

Notes

Introduction: Ukraine 2014

1. The AA provided for wide-ranging integration, short of EU membership. Complementing it was the Deep and Comprehensive Free Trade Area. Negotiations on a DCFTA agreement started in February 2008, and the text was initialed in July 2012.

2. "Agreement On Settlement Of Crisis In Ukraine—Full Text," *Guardian*, February 21, 2014.

3. Constitution of Ukraine (as amended in December 2004), http://legislationline.org/documents/action/popup/id/16258/preview. On the circumstances under which the referendum was conducted, see Ian Birrell, "Crimea's Referendum Was a Sham Display of Democracy," *Guardian*, March 17, 2014.

4. Office of the United Nations High Commissioner for Human Rights, "Report on the Human Rights Situations in Ukraine," September 16, 2014.

5. "As Kyiv Meets On Crisis, Rebel Claims Aid of Russian Troops," *New York Times*, August 28, 2014.

6. "Ukraine Crisis: NATO Plans East Bases To Counter Russia," *Guardian*, August 26, 2014, http://www.theguardian.com/world/2014/aug/26/nato-east-european-bases-counter-russian-threat.

1 The Making of Ukraine

1. James Marson, "Putin to the West: Hands Off Ukraine," *Time*, May 25, 2009.

2. Ralph S. Clem, "Why Eastern Ukraine Is An Integral Part of Ukraine," The Monkey Cage, Washingtonpost.com, March 7, 2014, http://www.washingtonpost.com/blogs/monkey-cage/wp/2014/03/07/why-eastern-ukraine-is-an-integral-part-of-ukraine/.

3. See Glen Kates, "Ukraine's East-West Divide: It's Not That Simple," Radio Free Europe/Radio Liberty, February 27, 2014, http://www.rferl.org/content/ukraine-east-west-divide/25279292.html.

4. "Crimean Parliament Approves Constitution," Associated Press, May 6, 1992, http://www.apnewsarchive.com/1992/Crimean-Parliament-Approves-Constitution/id-558835750cf19e2e340d948a157f19b1; "Crimean Parliament Votes to Back Independence from Ukraine," *New York Times*, May 6, 1992.

5. Details in Roman Solchanyk, *Ukraine and Russia: The Post-Soviet Transition* (Lanham, MD: Rowman and Littlefield, 2001), 138-139; Paul Kubicek, "Structure Agency and Secessionism in the Soviet Union and the Post-Soviet States," in Don Harrison Doyle, *Secession as an International Phenomenon: From America's Civil War to Contemporary Separatist Movements* (Athens: University of Georgia Press, 2010), 286-287; "Ukraine's Miners Bemoan the Costs of Independence," *New York Times*, July 17, 1993.

6. Roman Szporluk, *Russia, Ukraine, and the Breakup of the Soviet Union* (Stanford, CA: Hoover Institution Press, 2000), Ch. 15, "Ukraine: From an Imperial Periphery to a Sovereign State," 361-394. We reprise Szporluk's superb account and draw as well on Timothy Snyder, "Ukrainian Extremists Will Only Triumph if Russia Invades," *New Republic*, April 7, 2014, http://www.newrepublic.com/article/117395/historic-ukrainian-russian-relations-impact-maidan-revolution. For excellent histories of Ukraine, see Orest Subtelny, *Ukraine: A History*, Fourth Edition (Toronto: University of Toronto Press, 2009); Robert Paul Magocsi, *History of Ukraine*, Second Revised and Expanded Edition (Toronto: University of

Toronto Press, 2010); Serhy Yekelchik, *Ukraine: Birth of a Modern Nation* (New York: Oxford University Press, 2007). A brief overview appears in Anatol Lieven, *Russia and Ukraine: A Fraternal Rivalry* (Washington, DC, United States Institute of Peace, 1999), Ch. 1, "Russia and Ukraine: United and Divided By History," 11-48.

7. Halik Kochanski, *Eagle Unbowed: Poland and the Poles In the Second World War* (Cambridge, MA: Harvard University Press, 2012), 359.

8. For lucid accounts, see Timothy Snyder, *The Reconstruction of Nations: Poland, Ukraine, Lithuania, Belarus, 1569-1999* (New Haven: Yale University Press, 2003), Ch. 8; Magocsi, *History of Ukraine*, Chs. 48 and 49.

9. On Ukrainian Nazi collaborators in the killing of Jews and ethnic cleansing and murder of Poles during the German occupation, see Kochanski, *Eagle Unbowed*, 359-362.

10. Linda Kinstler, "Protestors in Eastern Ukraine Are Chanting 'Novorossiya,' A Term That's Back in Vogue," *New Republic*, April 7, 2014, http://www.newrepublic.com/article/117284/federalized-ukraine-could-mean-return-novorossiya. On Putin's use of this label, see "Away from Show of Diplomacy, Putin Puts on a Show of His Own," *New York Times*, April 17, 2014; Nick Robins-Early, "Here's Why Putin's Calling Ukraine 'Novorossiya, Is Important," *Huffington Post*, April 18, 2014, http://www.huffingtonpost.com/2014/04/18/putin-novorossiya-ukraine_n_5173559.html; Adam Taylor, "Novorossiya: The Latest Concept to Worry About in Ukraine," Washingtonpost.com, April 18, 2014, http://www.washingtonpost.com/blogs/worldviews/wp/2014/04/18/understanding-novorossiya-the-latest-historical-concept-to-get-worried-about-in-ukraine/; and "Prezident Rossii Vladimir Putin obratilsia k opolcheniiu Novorossii," Kremlin.ru, August 29, 2014, http://www.kremlin.ru/news/46506.

11. Adrian A. Basora and Aleksandr Fisher, "Putin's 'Greater Novorossiya'—The Dismemberment of Ukraine," *E-Notes*, Foreign Policy Research Institute, May 2014, http://www.fpri.org/articles/2014/05/putins-greater-novorossiya-dismemberment-ukraine.

12. See Serhiy Yekelchik, *Ukraine: Birth of a Modern Nation* (New York: Oxford University Press, 2007), Ch. 3, for details; and Taras Kuzio's elegant summary in *Ukrainian Security Policy* (Westport, CT: Praegar, 1995), 8-9.

13. On the Treaty of Riga and the events that laid the groundwork for it, see Kochanski, *Eagle Unbowed*, 17-21.

14. Moshe Lewin, *The Gorbachev Phenomenon: An Historical Interpretation*, Expanded Edition (Berkeley: University of California Press, 1991); Alexis de Tocqueville, *The Ancien Regime and the French Revolution* (London: Penguin, 2008).

15. Geoffrey A. Hosking, *Rulers and Victim: Russians and the Soviet Union* (Cambridge: Harvard University Press, 2006), 387.

16. Igor Filatochev and Roy Bradshaw, "The Soviet Hyperinflation: Its Origin and Impact Throughout the Former Republics," *Soviet Studies*, Vol. 44, No. 4 (1992), 739.

17. C.R. Neu, *Soviet International Finance in the Gorbachev Era* (Santa Monica, CA: Rand Corporation, 1991), v-vi.

18. Orest Subtelny, *Ukraine*, 589-591. Subtelny's discussion pertains to the immediate aftermath of independence but the economic ills he discusses were already evident in the final years of the Soviet Union.

19. Yekelchik, *Ukraine*, 184.

20. These efforts gathered momentum after independence but were evident during the Soviet twilight as well. See David Marples, *Heroes and Villains: Creating National History in Contemporary Ukraine*, Second Edition (Budapest: Central European University Press, 2009).

21. On the famine and the question of whether it constituted a genocide—a term then not yet born—see Robert Conquest, *Harvest of Sorrow: Soviet Collectivization and the Terror Famine* (Oxford: Oxford University Press, 1987). For documents and personal testimonies, see Bohdan Klid and Alexander J. Motyl, eds., *The Holodomor Reader: A Sourcebook on the Famine of 1932-1933 in Ukraine* (Alberta: Canadian Institute of Ukrai-

nian Studies, 2012). For a survivor's account, see Miron Dolot, *Execution By Hunger: The Hidden Holocaust* (New York: Norton, 1987).

22. On studies of the famine in the *glasnost'* period and the communist party's release of sensitive documents pointing to official culpability, see Stanislav Kulchytsky, "Why Did Stalin Eliminate the Ukrainians?" *Den'*, November 8, 2005, http://www.day.kiev.ua/en/article/history-and-i/why-did-stalin-exterminate-ukrainians-2

23. Details on the east-west division and the political trends in Crimea are from Yekelchik, *Ukraine*, 187-188, and United Nations High Commission for Refugees, "Chronology for Crimean Russians in Ukraine," Minorities at Risk Project (2014), http://www.refworld.org/docid/469f38ec2.html.

24. Taras Kuzio, *Ukraine: From Perestroika to Statehood,* Second Edition (New York: St. Martin's Press, 2000), 181-183.

25. For a vivid account of the Belovezh meeting see Serhii Plokhy, *The Last Empire: The Final Days of the Soviet Union* (New York: Basic Books, 2014), 297-316; quote on 299.

26. For an early and excellent assessment of newly independent Ukraine's challenges, see Alexander J. Motyl, *Dilemmas of Independence: Ukraine After Totalitarianism* (New York: Council on Foreign Relations, 1993). On the lack on consensus on identity and domestic and foreign policy, see the astute (and, in the case of Crimea, prescient) discussion in Taras Kuzio, *Ukrainian Security Policy* (Westport, CT: Praegar, 1995), 16-17.

27. On the short-lived West Ukrainian National Republic, see Subtelny, *Ukraine*, Chs. 18 and 19; Magocsi, *A History of Ukraine*, Ch. 41. The details of what happened in the Ukrainian-majority territories within the Habsburg and Russian empires are too complicated to recount here. Suffice it to say that, in addition to the short-lived West Ukrainian National Republic, there was a succession of equally ephemeral Ukrainian governments that emerged once the Tsarist Empire unraveled: the Ukrainian National Republic (proclaimed in January 1918 by the Ukrainian Central Rada or parliament that was established in March 1917),

the German-backed Hetmanate (April-November 1918), and the second Ukrainian National Republic (December 1918-late 1920)

28. The percentage is derived from the 1989 census. See Clem, "Why Eastern Ukraine is an Integral Part of Ukraine."

29. "Kravchuk and Yeltsin Strike Deal: On Fleet," *Moscow Times*, August 4, 1992.

30. Steven Pifer, "The Trilateral Process: The United States, Russia, Ukraine, and Nuclear Weapons," Brookings Institution, *Arms Control Series*, Paper No. 6, May 2011.

31. Council on Foreign Relations, "Budapest Memorandums on Security Assurances, 1994," December 5, 1994, http://www.cfr.org/arms-control-disarmament-and-nonproliferation/budapest-memorandums-security-assurances-1994/p32484

32. Anders Åslund, *How Ukraine Became a Market Economy* (Washington, DC: Peter G. Peterson Institute for International Economics, 2009), 58.

33. Raphael Shen, *Ukraine's Economic Reform: Obstacles, Errors, Lessons* (Westport, CT: Greenwood, 1996), 69-76.

34. World Bank, "Poverty in Ukraine," Report No. 15602-UA (June 27, 1996), 1-22.

35. Solchanyk, *Ukraine and Russia*, 70-71; "Ukrainians Elect a New President," *New York Times*, July 12, 1994. For the breakdown of the vote distribution by province, see "Ukraine Presidential Election 1994," Electoralgeography.com, n.d., http://www.electoralgeography.com/new/en/countries/u/ukraine/ukraine-presidential-election-1994.html.

36. On Kuchma and the Crimea, we rely on Subtelny, *Ukraine* 609-610; Yekelchik, *Ukraine* 201-201; and Taras Kuzio, "Autonomous Sentiment Stirring in Western Ukraine," *Kyiv Post,* August 2, 2002, http://www.taraskuzio.net/media13_files/8.pdf.

37. The details are from Alexander Cooley and Volodymyr Dubovik, "Will Sevastopol Survive? The Triangular Politics of Russia's Naval Base

in Crimea," PONARS Eurasia Policy Memo, No. 47 (2008), http://www. ponarseurasia.org/sites/default/files/policy-memos-pdf/pepm_047.pdf.

38. Kuzio, "Autonomous Sentiment."

39. North Atlantic Treaty Organization (NATO), July 9, 1997, "Charter on a Distinctive Partnership," http://www.nato.int/cps/en/natolive/official_texts_25457.htm: NATO, November 22, 2002, "NATO-Ukraine Action Plan," http://www.nato.int/cps/en/natolive/official_texts_19547.htm.

40. "Ukraine Not Ready to Join NATO: Kuchma," *EUBusiness*, June 2004, http://www.eubusiness.com/europe/ukraine/040614150428.yo1wvz3i; "Kuchma Cuts Accession to NATO, EU from Military Doctrine," *People's Daily*, July 27, 2004, http://english.peopledaily.com.cn/200407/27/eng20040727_150950.html; Vladimir Socor, "Ukraine Rephrases NATO Goal," Jamestown Foundation, *Eurasia Daily Monitor,* Vol. 1. No. 63 (July 29, 2004), http://www.jamestown.org/single/?tx_ttnews%5Btt_news%5D=26685&no_cache=1#.U8Z5yI1dUjE

41. "Kuchma: A CIS Integrator?" *Eurasia Daily Report*, Vol. 8, No. 56, March 20, 2002, http://www.jamestown.org/single/?tx_ttnews[tt_news]=24018&tx_ttnews[backPid]=216&no_cache=1; Roman Woronowycz, "Ukraine's President Elected Chair of CIS Council of Heads of State," *Ukrainian Weekly*, February 2, 2003, http://www. ukrweekly.com/old/archive/2003/050301.shtml.

42. Details are from International Monetary Fund (IMF), "Ukraine— Recent Economic Developments," Staff Country Report, No. 97/107 (October 1997); Åslund, *How Ukraine Became a Market Economy*, 68-83; and Robert Kravchuk, "Kuchma as Economic Reformer," *Problems of Post-Communism*, Vol. 52, No. 5 (September/October, 2005), 48.

43. Kravchuk, "Kuchma as Economic Reformer," Table 1, 50; World Bank, "GDP Growth Rate (annual %)," http://data.worldbank.org/indicator/NY.GDP.MKTP.KD.ZG?page=1&order=wbapi_data_value_2009%20wbapi_data_value%20wbapi_data_value-first&sort=asc.

44. "World's Biggest Steelmaker is Acquiring Ukrainian Mill, *New York Times*, October 25, 2005.

45. See the excellent discussion in Andrew Wilson, *The Ukrainians: Unexpected Nation,* Third Edition (New Haven: Yale University Press, 209), 259-274.

46. Andrew Wilson, "Ukraine's New Virtual Politics," *East European Constitutional Review*, Vol. 10, No. 60, (Spring/Summer 2001), 61.

47. Taras Kuzio, "Regime Type and Politics in Ukraine Under Kuchma," *Communist and Post Communist Studies*, Vol. 38 (2005), 174.

48. Keith Darden, "Blackmail as a Tool of Domination: Ukraine Under Kuchma," *East European Constitutional Review,* Vol. 10, No. 67 (Spring/Summer 2001), 67-71.

49. Lucan A. Way, "Kuchma's Failed Authoritarianism," *Journal of Democracy*, Vol. 16, No. 2 (April 2005), 132.

50. Radio Free Europe/Radio Liberty, March 3, 2005, "Transcript: What Do Melnychenko's Tapes Saw About the Gongadze Case?" http://www.rferl.org/content/article/1057789.html

51. An excellent analysis of the elections is offered in Taras Kuzio, "The 2002 Parliamentary Elections in Ukraine: Democratization or Authoritarianism?" *Journal of Communist Studies and Transitional Politics*, Vol. 19, No. 2 (June 2003), 24-54.

52. Kuzio, "The 2002 Parliamentary Elections," 26-27, 31-33, 46-50.

53. The best account is Andrew Wilson, *Ukraine's Orange Revolution* (New Haven: Yale University Press, 2005).

54. "Threat to Split Ukraine in Two As Crisis Grows," *Guardian*, November 28, 2004: Peter Lavelle, "Analysis: Ultimatum in Ukraine," *United Press International*, November 29, 2004, http://www.upi.com/Business_News/Security-Industry/2004/11/29/Analysis-Ultimatum-in-Ukraine/UPI-96121101747439/.

55. See Volodymyr Kulyk, "Language Policy and Language Attitudes in Post-Orange Ukraine," in Juliane Besters-Dilger, ed., *Language Policy and* [sic] *Language Situation in Ukraine: Analysis and Recommendations* (New York: Peter Lang, 2009), 23, and "The Orange Revolution," *Time*,

November 28, 2004. On the east-west divide, also see Taras Kuzio, "From Kuchma to Yushchenko: Ukraine's 2004 Political Elections and the Orange Revolution," *Problems of Post-Communism*, Vol. 52, No. 2 (March/April 2005), 29-44.

56. Mark R. Beissinger, "Why We Should Be Sober About the Long-Term Prospects of Democracy in Ukraine, *Washington Post*, March 11, 2014.

57. Oleksandr Sushko and Olena Prystayko, "Western Influence," and Nikolai Petrov and Andrei Ryabov, "Russia's Role in the Orange Revolution," Chs. 7 and 8 respectively, in Anders Åslund and Michael McFaul, eds., *Revolution in Orange: The Origins of Ukraine's Democratic Breakthrough* (Washington, DC: Carnegie Endowment for International Peace, 2006). Quote from Petrov and Ryabov, 145.

58. "Putin Uses Soft Power to Restore Russian Empire," *New York Times*, November 14, 2004; "Supporters of President-Elect Push Back," *New York Times*, November 28, 2004.

59. Katja Richters, *The Post-Soviet Russian Orthodox Church: Politics, Culture and Greater Russia* (New York: Routledge, 2012), 115-117; "Ukraine's Opposition Girds for Runoff Vote," *Washington Post,* December 6, 2004.

60. Paul Kubicek, "Problems of Post-Post-Communism: Ukraine After the Orange Revolution," *Democratization*, Vol. 16, No. 2 (April 2009), 324.

61. "Fired Ukrainian Prime Minister Sees End of 'Orange Revolution' Unity," *New York Times*, September 10, 2005.

62. For details, see Wilson, *The Ukrainians*, 326-328.

63. See Wilson, *The Ukrainians*, 328-333.

64. Marek Gora, Oleksandr Rohozynovsky, and Oxana Sinyavskaya, "Pension Reform Options for Russia and Ukraine: A Critical Analysis of Available Options and Their Expected Outcomes," Center for Social and Economic Research, ESCIRRU (Economic and Social Consequences of Industrial Restructuring in Russia and Ukraine) Working Paper No. 25, February 2010. For policies reflecting the lack of a coherent strategy and divisions within the government, see also Yevgen Zinovyev, "The Politi-

cal and Economic Environment in Ukraine," in Marat Terterov, ed., *Ukraine Since the Orange Revolution: A Business and Investment Review* (Edinburgh; GMB Publishing, 2006) and Anders Åslund, "The Economic Policy of Ukraine After the Orange Revolution," *Eurasian Geography and Economics*, Vol. 46, No. 5 (2005), 342-347.

65. Industrial output dropped by 30 percent in 2005–2009 because of diminished demand at home and abroad and cutbacks in bank lending. The retail and agriculture sectors also suffered a slowdown but were hit less hard. The data on the Ukrainian economy following the Orange Revolution are derived from IMF, "Ukraine: Second Review Under the Stand-By Arrangement and Request for Modification of Performance Criteria," Country Report 09/270, September 2009; and IMF, https://www.imf.org/external/pubs/ft/scr/2009/cr09270.pdf and "Ukraine: 2012 Article IV Consultation," Country Report 12/315, November 2012, https://www.imf.org/external/pubs/ft/scr/2012/cr12315.pdf

66. "Ukraine: Unemployment Rate: 2004 to 2014," Statista.com, http://www.statista.com/statistics/296132/ukraine-unemployment-rate/.

67. "The Global Debt Clock," Economist.com, http://www.economist.com/content/global_debt_clock.

68. "In Ukraine, The Death of the Orange Revolution," *Time*, February 3, 2010; Transparency International "Corruption Perceptions Index," http://www.transparency.org/research/cpi/overview.

69. Victor Yushchenko, "Georgia and the Stakes for Ukraine," *Washington Post*, August 25, 2008.

70. Taras Kuzio, "Ukraine Tightens the Screws in Sevastopol," *Eurasia Daily Monitor*, Vol. 6, No. 141 (July 23, 2009), http://www.jamestown.org/single/?no_cache=1&tx_ttnews%5Btt_news%5D=35304&tx_ttnews%5BbackPid%5D=7&cHash=1eb3ea7121#.U8aE1Y1dUjE

71. For the text, see US Department of State, Bureau of European and Eurasian Affairs, "United States-Ukraine Charter on Strategic Partnership," December 19, 2008, http://www.state.gov/p/eur/rls/or/142231.htm.

72. Viktor Yushchenko, "The Holodomor," *Wall Street Journal,* November 26, 2007, http://online.wsj.com/news/articles/SB119602928167703 318.

73. "To the President of Ukraine Viktor Andreyevich Yuschenko [sic]," President of Russia, Official Web Portal, August 11, 2009, http://archive. kremlin.ru/eng/text/docs/209178.shtml; "Bipolar Holodomor," *Kommersant,* November 17, 2008, http://archive.kremlin.ru/eng/text/ docs/2009/08/220759.shtml. See also "Yushchenko Brings Stalin to Court Over Genocide, RT.com, April 29, 2010, http://rt.com/politics/ holodomor-famine-stalin-ukraine/

74. "President Demands Resuming Halted Construction of Mazepa Monument in Poltava," August 25, 2009, http://www.president.gov.ua/ en/news/14764.html.

75. Andreas Kappeler, "The Politics of History in Contemporary Ukraine: Russia, Poland, Austria, and Europe," in Juliane Besters-Dilger, ed., *Ukraine On Its War to Europe: Interim Results of the Orange Revolution* (New York: Peter Lang, 2009), 220-22; "Ukraine and Russia Clash at Poltava," *Kommersant,* March 26, 2008, http://www.kommersant.com/p871344/ r_1/Battle_of_Poltava/.

76. A Mazepa monument was not built at Poltava or Kyiv. There are two—one in Chernihiv and the other at his one-time capital, Baturyn— but neither bears his name. Thanks to Alexander Motyl for clarifying this. Mazepa's visage does adorn Ukraine's 10-hryvnia note.

77. On the controversy over Mazepa and other historical personalities and episodes during this period, see Juliane Besters-Dilger, ed., *Ukraine On Its Way to Europe: Interim Results of the Orange Revolution* (New York: Peter Lang, 2009), 220-23; Adrian Karatnycky and Alexander J. Motyl, "Poltava and Mazepa," *Wall Street Journal* (Europe), July 8, 2009.

78. See "Factbox: Russia's Energy Disputes With Ukraine and Belarus," Reuters, December 12, 2012, http://www.reuters.com/article/2012/ 12/21/us-russia-gas-disputes-idUSBRE8BK11T20121221; "Ukraine, In Rebuke to Russia, Says It Has Right to Take Gas," *New York Times*, Janu-

ary 3, 2006; Jonathan Stern, "The Russian-Ukrainian Gas Crisis of 2006," Oxford Institute for Energy Studies, January 16, 2006.

79. The details of the Russia-Ukraine gas trade are devilishly complex and can be offered here only in bare summary. Our account of the 2009 crisis and its background relies heavily on the superb explanation provided by Simon Pirani, Jonathan Stern, and Katja Yefimava, in "The Russo-Ukrainian Gas Dispute of 2009: A Comprehensive Assessment," Oxford Institute for Energy Studies, February 2009.

80. On the 2010 election and its immediate aftermath, see Olexiy Haran and Dmytro Prokopchuk, "The Drama of Ukraine 2010 Presidential Election," *Ponars Eurasia Policy Memo*, No. 89, March 2010, https://www.gwu.edu/~ieresgwu/assets/docs/pepm_089.pdf.

81. Dominique Arel, "Double-Talk: Why Ukrainians Fight Over Language," *Foreign Affairs*, March 18, 2014, http://www.foreignaffairs.com/articles/141042/dominique-arel/double-talk. See the map depicting the 2010 presidential election's second round vote distribution in Sergiy Kudelia, "Ukraine 2014 Presidential Election Result Is Unlikely to be Repeated, Monkey Cage, WashingtonPost.com, June 2, 2104, http://www.washingtonpost.com/blogs/monkey-cage/wp/2014/06/02/ukraines-2014-presidential-election-result-is-unlikely-to-be-repeated/.

82. For a profile, see "Viktor Yanukovych," *Moscow Times*, n.d., http://www.themoscowtimes.com/mt_profile/viktor_yanukovych/433767.html.

83. "Yanukovych Reverses Ukraine's Position on Holodomor Famine," RIA Novosti, April 27, 2010, http://en.ria.ru/exsoviet/20100427/158772431.html.

84. "Ukraine Votes to Abandon NATO Ambitions," BBC News, June 3, 2010, http://www.bbc.com/news/10229626.

85. "Ukrainians Protest Against Russian Language Law," *Guardian*, July 4, 2012; "Ukrainians Polarized Over Language Law," BBC News, July 5, 2012, http://www.bbc.com/news/world-europe-18725849.

86. Arel, "Double-Talk." Stephen Pifer and Hannah Thoburn, "What Ukraine's New Language Law Means for National Unity," Brookings Institution, *Up Front*, August 21, 2012, http://www.brookings.edu/blogs/up-front/posts/2012/08/21-ukraine-language-pifer-thoburn.

87. For a map that provides a breakdown by province of those in Ukraine who identify Russian as their native language, see, "Ukrainians Who Identify as Ethnic Russians Or Say Russian Is Their First Language," Radio Free Europe/Radio Liberty, July 17, 2014, http://www.rferl.org/contentinfographics/map-ukraine-percentage-who-identify-as-ethnic-russians-or-say-russian-is-their-first-language-/25323841.html.

88. For details on politics under Yanukovych, see Rajan Menon and Alexander J. Motyl, "Counterrevolution in Kiev: Hopes Fade for Ukraine," *Foreign Affairs*, Vol. 90, No. 6 (October/November 2011), 137-148; Alexander J. Motyl, "Ukrainian Blues," *Foreign Affairs* (July/August 2010), http://www.foreignaffairs.com/articles/66447/alexander-j-motyl/ukrainian-blues; Serhiy Kudelia, "Ukraine in Context: What Happens When Authoritarians Fall," *Foreign Affairs*, February 27, 2014, http://www.foreignaffairs.com/articles/140976/serhiy-kudelia/ukraine-in-context;

89. "Rada to Introduce Criminal Responsibility for Slander," *Kyiv Post,* September 18, 2012, http://www.kyivpost.com/content/ukraine/rada-to-introduce-criminal-responsibility-for-slander-313141.html.

90. Transparency International, "Corruption Perceptions Index 2013," http://www.transparency.org/cpi2013/results.

91. Steven Woehrel, "Ukraine: Current Issues and U.S. Policy," Congressional Research Service, May 11, 2011, 4; Nazar Kholod, "Reforming the Economy Under Yanukovych: The First Two Years," Carnegie Endowment for International Peace, April 2, 2012, http://carnegieendowment.org/2012/04/02/reforming-ukrainian-economy-under-yanukovych-first-two-years/a63h.

92. "Viktor Yanukovych Boasted About Corruption, Says Mikheil Saakashvili," *Guardian*, February 25, 2014.

93. For the text, as translated and republished by the Ukraine-US Business Council on September 10, 2010, see: http://www.usubc.org/site/files/Ukraine_Program_of_Economic_Reforms_2010-2014.pdf.

94. Anders Åslund, "The Management of Ukraine's Economy Under Yanukovych," Meeting Summary, Chatham House, April 23, 2012, http://www.chathamhouse.org/publications/papers/view/183261.

95. World Bank, "GNI Per Capita Ranking, Atlas Method and PPP Based,"http://data.worldbank.org/data-catalog/GNI-per-capita-Atlas-and-PPP-table.

96. See the table in World Bank, "GDP Growth (Annual %)," http://data.worldbank.org/indicator/NY.GDP.MKTP.KD.ZG

97. Slawomir Matuszak and Arkadiusz Sarna, "From Stability to Stagnation," *Point of View* (Centre for Eastern Studies, Warsaw), No. 3 (March 2013), 6.

98. For details on Yanukovych's economic policies, see Matuszak and Sarna, "From Stability to Stagnation"; Woehrel, *Ukraine*; Kholod, "Reforming the Ukrainian Economy."

99. If that meant that the IMF would stop disbursements from its new July 2010 $15.5 billion credit line—it replaced the 2008 loan, also suspended because the promised reforms were not delivered—then so be it. That is in fact what happened in 2011, and Ukraine was left to handle $9.1 billion in payments to foreign creditors, the IMF included, in 2013, $3 billion more than it owed in 2012. The unwillingness to adopt reform that would hurt millions of people of modest means was understandable, even if the guiding principle was not compassion. The drawback was that budget imbalances continued as pension payments and expensive energy subsidies (covering half the purchase price) consumed government revenue. "Yanukovych Pledges to Name New Prime Minister Soon as IMF Talks Loom," *Kyiv Post*, December 7, 2012, http://www.kyivpost.com/content/ukraine/ukraine-leader-pledges-to-name-pm-soon-as-imf-talks-loom-317304.html.

100. For a comprehensive and detailed assessment of Ukraine's energy sector and its problems, see International Energy Agency, *Ukraine 2012* (Paris: IEA/OECD, 2012).

101. None of these measures began to address genuine solutions to Ukraine's energy bind. Ukraine uses more than three times as much energy per unit of GDP than the OECD average. Increasing energy efficiency would require difficult reforms, including a phaseout of subsidies and the modernization of Ukraine's buildings and industries, most of which predate the 1970s. Ukraine also has abundant reserves of conventional and unconventional gas reserves (shale and coalbed methane). They could be tapped, but not without foreign investment, which would require attacking corruption and ensuring the rule of law.

102. See European Commission, "EU-Ukraine Deep and Comprehensive Free Trade Area," n.d., trade.ec.europa.eu/doclib/html/150981.htm; European Union, External Action Service, "EU-Ukraine Association Agreement—The Complete Texts," n.d., http://eeas.europa.eu/ukraine/assoagreement/assoagreement-2013_en.htm.

2   Nobody Expected a Crisis

1. Gregory Feifer, "Unloved but Unbowed, Ukraine's Viktor Yushchenko Leaves Office," RFE/RL, February 24, 2010, http://www.rferl.org/content/Unloved_But_Unbowed_Ukraines_Viktor_Yushchenko_Leaves_Office/1967436.html.

2. Luke Harding, "Yanukovych Set to Become President as Observers Say Ukraine Election Was Fair," *Guardian*, February 8, 2010, http://www.theguardian.com/world/2010/feb/08/viktor-yanukovych-ukraine-president-election.

3. Adrian Karatnicky, "Re-introducing Viktor Yanukovych," *Wall Street Journal*, February 7, 2010, http://online.wsj.com/news/articles/SB100014240527487034277045750512532474925 16.

4. The International Republican Institute, Public Opinion Survey, Residents of Ukraine October 30–November 11, 2011, http://www.iri.org/sites/default/files/2012%20January%2026%20Survey%20of%20Ukrai-

nian%20Public%20Opinion%2C%20October%2030-November%20
11%2C%202011.pdf.

5. "Yulia Tymoshenko's Trials," *Economist*, October 15, 2011, http://
www.economist.com/node/21532290.

6. David Hershenzon, "Obserers Denounce Ukrainian Election, Citing
Abuses by Rulers," *New York Times*, October 29, 2012, http://www.
nytimes.com/2012/10/30/world/europe/international-observers-
denounce-ukrainian-election.html?_r=1&.

7. "Ukraine Opposition Alleges Election Fraud," *Al Jazeera*, November 6,
2012, http://www.aljazeera.com/news/europe/2012/11/2012115134229
319119.html.

8. Benjamin Bidder, "Profiting from Power? The Dubious Business of
the Yanukovych Clan," *Spiegel Online International*, May 16, 2012, http://
www.spiegel.de/international/world/the-dubious-businees-of-ukraine-
president-yanukovych-and-his-clan-a-833127.html.

9. The International Republic 'institute, Public Opinion Survey, Residents of Ukraine October 30–November 11, 2011, http://www.iri.org/
sites/default/files/2012%20January%2026%20Survey%20of%20Ukrai-
nian%20Public%20Opinion%2C%20October%2030-November%20
11%2C%202011.pdf.

10. Sergii Leshchenko, "The two worlds of Viktor Yanukovych's
Ukraine," Opendemocracy.net, March 14, 2013, https://www.opendem-
ocracy.net/od-russia/sergii-leshchenko/two-worlds-of-viktor-
yanukovych's-ukraine.

11. "Khoroshkovskiy Quits, Blasts Azarov," *Kyiv Post*, December 14,
2012, http://www.kyivpost.com/content/politics/ukraine-government-
no2-quits-blasts-azarov-317669.html.

12. Christoher J. Miller, "Media Grab," *Kyiv Post*, June 27, 2013, http://
www.kyivpost.com/content/ukraine/media-grab-326233.html.

13. "Ukrainian Oligarchs: The First Steps," *Ukrainian Week*, August 19,
2011, http://ukrainianweek.com/Economics/29575.

14. "Profile: Ukraine's President Petro Poroshenko," BBC News, June 7, 2014, http://www.bbc.com/news/world-europe-26822741.

15. "Yanukovych and Oligarchs: A Short or Long-Term Relationship?", *Kyiv Post*, November 11, 2010, http://www.kyivpost.com/opinion/op-ed/yanukovych-and-oligarchs-a-short-or-long-term-rela-89559.html.

16. "The Dictator of a Pluralistic Country," *Economist*, October 27, 2012, http://www.economist.com/news/europe/21565232-sense-national-defeatism-may-let-president-viktor-yanukovych-stay-power-dictator.

17. Christian Neef, "Yanukovych's Fall: The Power of Ukraine's Billionaires," *Spiegel Online*, February 25, 2014, http://www.spiegel.de/international/europe/how-oligarchs-in-ukraine-prepared-for-the-fall-of-yanukovych-a-955328.html.

18. Andrew Rettman, "Media Crackdown Ahead of EU-Ukraine summit," *EU Observer*, February 21, 2013, http://euobserver.com/foreign/119140.

19. "IRI Releases Pre-Parliamentary Elections Survey of Ukrainian Public Opinion," International Republic Institute, January 26, 2012. http://www.iri.org/news-events-press-center/news/iri-releases-pre-parliamentary-elections-survey-ukrainian-public-opini.

20. C.J. Chivers, "How Top Spies in Ukraine Changed the Nation's Path," *New York Times*, January 17, 2005, http://www.nytimes.com/2005/01/17/international/europe/17ukraine.html?pagewanted=print&_r=2&.

21. "Party of Regions Gets 185 Seats in Ukrainian Parliament, Batkivschyna 101 – CEC," Interfax-Ukraine, November 12, 2012, http://en.interfax.com.ua/news/general/126937.html.

22. "Why Is Ukraine's Economy in Such a Mess?", *Economist*, March 5, 2014, http://www.economist.com/blogs/freeexchange/2014/03/ukraine-and-russia.

23. Edward Chow and Jonathan Elkind, "Where East Meets West: European Gas and Ukrainian Reality," *Washington Quarterly*, January 2009.

24. Roman Olearchyk, "Russia Lowers Ukraine Gas Prices," *Financial Times*, April 21, 2010.

25. "Ukraine Plans to Pay Gas Debt to Russia by End-2013," Interfax-Ukraine, November 18, 2013, http://en.interfax.com.ua/news/economic/175417.html.

26. "Ukraine Has $3.3Bln Unpaid Gas Bill – Gazprom," RIA Novosti, February 3, 2014, http://en.ria.ru/russia/20140203/187164045/Ukraines-Gas-Debt-to-Russia-Rising--Report.html.

27. "Experts Calling on Ukraine to Cancel Hrvynia's Pegging to Dollar," *Kyiv Post*, December 7, 2011, http://www.kyivpost.com/content/business/experts-calling-on-ukraine-to-cancel-hryvnias-pegg-118345.html.

28. "Yanukovych Boots Social Spending Ahead of Ukraine Vote," RIA Novosti, April 16, 2012, http://en.ria.ru/business/20120416/172857161.html.

29. "Yanukovych Kicks Off His 'Big Lender' Tour: First Stop China, Next Russia," *Russia Today*, December 3, 2013, http://rt.com/business/ukraine-yanukovych-china-trip-647/.

30. Jonathan Stearns, "EU Offers Ukraine Millions in Trade Aid to Steady Economy," Bloomberg, March 11, 2014, http://www.bloomberg.com/news/2014-03-11/eu-offers-ukraine-millions-in-trade-aid-to-steady-economy.html.

31. Kateryna Choursina, "Ukraine Rating Cut to Greek Level by S&P as Devaluation Seen," Bloomberg, November 1, 2013, http://www.bloomberg.com/news/2013-11-01/ukraine-rating-cut-to-b-by-s-p-as-devaluation-seen-more-likely.html.

32. Adrian Karatnycky, "Ukraine's New President Viktor Yanukovych is No Threat to Democracy," *American Interest*, November 1, 2010, http://www.the-american-interest.com/articles/2010/11/01/orange-peels/.

33. Steven Pifer and William Taylor, "Yanukovich's First Year," *New York Times*, March 1, 2011, http://www.nytimes.com/2011/03/02/opinion/02iht-edpifer02.html.

34. Pavel Korduban, "Ukraine Fails to Secure IMF Financing in 2011," *Eurasia Daily Monitor*, November 16, 2011, http://www.jamestown.org/single/?tx_ttnews%5Btt_news%5D=38678&no_cache=1#.U_3Q1Uu4nlJ.

35. Luke Harding, "Ukraine extends lease for Russia's Black Sea Fleet," *Guardian*, April 21, 2010, http://www.theguardian.com/world/2010/apr/21/ukraine-black-sea-fleet-russia.

36. "Poor Ukrainian-Russian Ties Reflect Yanukovych-Putin Relationship," *Eurasia Daily Monitor*, September 30, 2011, http://www.refworld.org/docid/4e8d75502.html.

37. Pavel Korduban, "Yanukovych and Tymoshenko Courting Moscow Ahead of Election," *Eurasia Daily Monitor*, September 9, 2009, http://www.jamestown.org/single/?tx_ttnews%5Btt_news%5D=35462&no_cache=1#.U72VXxa4nlI.

38. Carol Matlack, "Putin's Eurasian Union Looks Like a Bad Deal, Even for Russia," *Bloomberg Businessweek*, May 29, 2014, http://www.businessweek.com/articles/2014-05-29/putins-eurasian-union-looks-like-a-bad-deal-even-for-russia.

39. Central Intelligence Agency, *World Factbook*, 2014, https://www.cia.gov/library/publications/the-world-factbook/geos/up.html.

40. "Information on the EU-Ukraine Association Agreement," European Union External Action. http://eeas.europa.eu/top_stories/2012/140912_ukraine_en.htm.

41. Štefan Füle, "Statement on the Pressure Exercised by Russia on Countries of the Eastern Partnership," Europa.eu, September 11, 2013, http://europa.eu/rapid/press-release_SPEECH-13-687_en.htm.

42. Christopher J. Miller, "Yanukovych's Secret Meeting with Putin Raises Questions of Customs Union Promise," *Kyiv Post*, December 7, 2013, http://www.kyivpost.com/content/ukraine/yanukovychs-secret-meeting-with-putin-raises-questions-of-customs-union-promise-333211.html.

43. Kathy Lally, "Deposed Yanukovych Wants Russia to Give Crimea Back to Ukraine," *Washington Post*, April 2, 2014, http://www.washing-

tonpost.com/world/deposed-yanukovych-wants-russia-to-give-crimea-back-to-ukraine/2014/04/02/e37124b6-561b-45c6-9390-a0d7d346ded6_story.html.

44. Steven Pifer, "Developments in Ukraine and Implications for U.S. Policy," Brookings Institution, February 1, 2012, http://www.brookings.edu/research/testimony/2012/02/01-ukraine-pifer.

45. Vladimir Socor, "Ukraine's Top Three Leaders Request NATO Membership Action Plan," *Eurasia Daily Monitor*, January 18, 2008, http://www.jamestown.org/single/?tx_ttnews%5Btt_news%5D=33304&no_cache=1#.U_34pEu4nlJ.

46. "Bucharest Summit Declaration," North Atlantic Treaty Organization, April 3, 2008. http://www.nato.int/cps/en/natolive/official_texts_8443.htm.

47. "Ukraine's Parliament Votes to Abandon NATO Ambitions," BBC News, June 3, 2010, http://www.bbc.com/news/10229626.

48. Julie Ray and Neli Esipova, "Before Crisis, Ukrainians More Likely to See NATO as a Threat," *Gallup World*, March 14, 2014, http://www.gallup.com/poll/167927/crisis-ukrainians-likely-nato-threat.aspx.

49. "Crimean communists to protest against NATO's Sea Breeze exports," *Kyiv Post*, May 27, 2010, http://www.kyivpost.com/content/ukraine/crimean-communists-to-protest-against-natos-sea-br.html?flavour=full.

50. Zbigniew Brzezinski, *The Grand Chessboard: American Primacy and Its Geostrategic Imperatives* (Basic Books, New York, NY, 1997).

51. "Ukraine's Parliament Votes to Abandon NATO Ambitions," BBC News, June 3, 2010, http://www.bbc.com/news/10229626.

52. "What is the European Neighbourhood Policy," European Union External Action, http://eeas.europa.eu/enp/about-us/index_en.htm

53. Rikard Jozwiak, "Explainer: What Exactly Is An EU Association Agreement?", Radio Free Europe/Radio Liberty, November 20, 2013,

http://www.rferl.org/content/eu-association-agreement-explained/25174247.html.

54. David Cadier, "Is the European Neighbourhood Policy a Substitute for Enlargement?", London School of Economics, http://www.lse.ac.uk/IDEAS/publications/reports/pdf/SR018/Cadier_D.pdf.

55. Agnieszka K. Cianciara, "'Eastern Partnership'—Opening a New Chapter of Polish Eastern Policy and the European Neighbourhood Policy?", Institute of Public Affairs, June 2008, http://isp.org.pl/files/867 92010407036671001213792577.pdf.

56. Gunilla Herolf, "Sweden in Favour of Enlargements and Co-Initiator of the Eastern Partnership," Stockholm International Peace Research Institute, http://www.eu-28watch.org/?q=node/677.

57. "Joint Statement by Foreign Ministers Radek Sikorski and Carl Bildt," Ministry of Foreign Affairs, Republic of Poland, December 1, 2013, http://www.msz.gov.pl/en/news/joint_statement_by_foreign_ministers_radek_sikorski_and_carl_bildt_of_poland_and_sweden.

58. Christopher Alessi, "Tymoshenko Release: Ukraine's Geopolitical Future Hangs on Deal," *Spiegel Online*, October 30, 2013, http://www.spiegel.de/international/europe/tymoshenko-release-could-pave-way-for-eu-ukraine-trade-deal-a-930917.html.

59. Tonya Tumanova, "Yulia Tymoshenko to the EU leaders: Sign the AA with Ukraine If Viktor Yanukovych Agrees (the text of the address)," Ukrainian National News, November 27, 2013, http://www.unn.com.ua/en/news/1277270-yu-timoshenko-lideram-yes-pidpishit-ua-z-ukrayinoyu-yakscho-v-yanukovich-pogoditsya-tekst-zvernennya.

60. Serhiy Kudelia, "When External Leverage Fails: The Case of Yulia Tymoshenko's Trial," *Problems of Post-Communism*, January/February 2013, http://www.academia.edu/3080463/When_External_Leverage_Fails_The_Case_of_Yulia_Tymoshenkos_Trial.

61. Philip Zelikow and Condleezza Rice, *Germany Unified and Europe Transformed* (Cambridge, MA: Harvard University Press, 1995), 179–185.

62. "Putin's Prepared Remarks at 43rd Munuch Conference on Security Policy," *Washington Post*, February 12, 2007, http://www.washington-post.com/wp-dyn/content/article/2007/02/12/AR2007021200555.html.

63. Conversation, senior Russian national security official, July 18, 2014, Moscow.

64. Dmitri Trenin, in *Central Asia: Views from Washington, Moscow, and Beijing* (New York: ME Sharpe, 2007), 81.

65. Paul Reynolds, "New Russian World Order: The Five Principles," BBC News, September 1, 2008. http://news.bbc.co.uk/2/hi/europe/7591610.stm

66. Ivan Nechepurenko, "Putin Lashes Out Against Cold War–Style Containment of Russia," *Moscow Times*, July 1, 2014, http://www.the-moscowtimes.com/news/article/putin-lashes-out-against-cold-war-style-containment-of-russia/502817.html.

67. Leon Neyfakh, "Putin's Long Game? Meet the Eurasian Union," *Boston Globe*, March 9, 2014, http://www.bostonglobe.com/ideas/2014/03/09/putin-long-game-meet-eurasian-union/1eKLXEC3TJfzqK54elX5fL/story.html; Robert Coalson, "Putin's Return to Kremlin Could Boost Eurasian Union Project," *Voice of America*, March 8, 2012,http://www.voanews.com/content/putins-return-to-kremlin-could-reenergize-eurasian-union-project-142051333/180797.html.

68. Jon Henley, "A Brief Primer on Vladimir Putin's Eurasian Dream," February 18, 2014, http://www.theguardian.com/world/shortcuts/2014/feb/18/brief-primer-vladimir-putin-eurasian-union-trade.

69. Elena Mazneva, "EU Drafts $2.5 Billion Ukraine Gas Debt As Cuts Looms," *Bloomberg*, May 27, 2014.

70. Olga Shumylo-Tapiola, "Ukraine at the Crossroads: Between the EU DCFTA & Customs Union," IFRI, Russia/NIS Center, April 2012; Oleksandr Sushko, "A Fork in the Road? Ukraine between EU Association and Eurasian Customs Union," *Ponars Eurasia Policy Memos*, Policy Memo #293, September 2013, http://www.ponarseurasia.org/memo/fork-road-ukraine-between-eu-association-and-eurasian-customs-union.

71. Irina Reznik and Henry Meyer, "Russia Offers Ukraine Cheaper Gas to Join Moscow-Led Group," *Bloomberg*, December 2, 2013, http://www.bloomberg.com/news/2013-12-01/russia-lures-ukraine-with-cheaper-gas-to-join-moscow-led-pact.html.

72. Olga Shumylo-Tapiola, "Ukraine at the Crossroads: between the EU DCFTA & Customs Union," IFRI, Russia/NIS Center, April 2012; Oleksandr Sushko, "A Fork in the Road? Ukraine between EU Association and Eurasian Customs Union," *Ponars Eurasia Policy Memos*, Policy Memo #293, September 2013, http://www.ponarseurasia.org/memo/fork-road-ukraine-between-eu-association-and-eurasian-customs-union.

73. Steven Pifer, "Ukraine's Yanukovych Caught between Russia and the European Union," *World Politics Review*, October 23, 2013, http://www.worldpoliticsreview.com/articles/13324/ukraine-s-yanukovych-caught-between-russia-and-the-european-union.

74. Reuters, "Ukraine Signs for Observer Status in Customs Union," *Moscow Times*, June 3, 2013, http://www.themoscowtimes.com/business/article/ukraine-signs-for-observer-status-in-customs-union/480918.html.

75. Putin's Adviser Threatens Loss of Observer Status in Customs Union If Ukraine Signs Trade Treaty with Europe," *Kyiv Post*, June 14, 2013, http://www.kyivpost.com/content/ukraine/putins-adviser-threatens-loss-of-observer-status-in-customs-union-if-ukraine-signs-trade-treaty-with-europe-325639.html.

76. Roman Olearchyk, "Russia Accused of Triggering Trade War with Ukraine," *Financial Times*, August 15, 2013, http://www.ft.com/intl/cms/s/0/99068c0e-0595-11e3-8ed5-00144feab7de.html#axzz38hCBDX00; "Trading Insults," *Economist*, August 24, 2013, http://www.economist.com/news/europe/21583998-trade-war-sputters-tussle-over-ukraines-future-intensifies-trading-insults.

77. Ibid.

78. Ian Traynor and Oksana Grytsenko, "Ukraine Suspends Talks on EU Trade Pact as Putin Wins Tug of War," *Guardian*, November 21, 2013,

http://www.theguardian.com/world/2013/nov/21/ukraine-suspends-preparations-eu-trade-pact.

79. "Putin's Gambit: How the EU Lost Ukraine," *Der Spiegel*, November 25, 2013, http://www.spiegel.de/international/europe/how-the-eu-lost-to-russia-in-negotiations-over-ukraine-trade-deal-a-935476.html.

80. Ian Traynor and Oksana Grytsenko, "Ukraine Suspends Talks on EU Trade Pact as Putin Wins Tug of War," *Guardian*, November 21, 2013, http://www.theguardian.com/world/2013/nov/21/ukraine-suspends-preparations-eu-trade-pact.

81. Darina Marchak, Katya Gorchinskaya, "Russia Gives Ukraine Cheap Gas, \$15 Billion in Loans," *Kyiv Post*, December 17, 2013, http://www.kyivpost.com/content/ukraine/russia-gives-ukraine-cheap-gas-15-billion-in-loans-333852.html; "Russia's Emergency Loan to Ukraine on Hold Until Gov't Forms," *Russia Today*, January 30, 2014, http://rt.com/business/russia-loan-ukraine-postpone-401/.

82. The International Republican Institute, Public Opinion Survey, Residents of Ukraine, August 27–September 9, 2013. http://www.iri.org/sites/default/files/IRI_Ukraine_August-September_2013_Edited%20Poll.pdf.

83. Oksna Grytsenko, "Ukrainian Protesters Flood Kiev After President Pulls Out of the EU deal," *Guardian*, November 24, 2013. http://www.theguardian.com/world/2013/nov/24/ukraine-protesters-yanukovych-aborts-eu-deal-russia; "Huge Ukraine Rally over EU Agreement Delay," BBC, November 24, 2013. http://www.bbc.com/news/world-europe-25078952.

84. Oksana Grytsenko, "Ukraine's Bloody Crackdown Leads to Calls for Sanctions," *Guardian*, November 30, 2013, http://www.theguardian.com/world/2013/nov/30/ukraine-bloody-backlash-sanctions-eu.

85. BBC, "Ukraine Crisis Timeline," http://www.bbc.com/news/world-middle-east-26248275.

86. http://www.state.gov/secretary/remarks/2013/12/218585.htm.

87. BBC, "Ukraine Crisis Timeline," http://www.bbc.com/news/world-middle-east-26248275; BBC, "Parliament Abolishes Anti-Protest Law," January 28, 2014, http://www.bbc.com/news/world-europe-25923199.

88. BBC, "Ukraine Crisis Timeline," http://www.bbc.com/news/world-middle-east-26248275.

89. BBC, "Ukraine Crisis Timeline," http://www.bbc.com/news/world-middle-east-26248275.

90. "Agreement on the Settlement of Crisis in Ukraine—full text," *Guardian*, February 21, 2014, http://www.theguardian.com/world/2014/feb/21/agreement-on-the-settlement-of-crisis-in-ukraine-full-text.

91. BBC, "Ukraine Crisis Timeline," http://www.bbc.com/news/world-middle-east-26248275.

92. Conversation with a senior Russian official, Moscow, July 17, 2014.

93. Shaun Walker, "Ukraine: Vladimir Putin Lays Blame at Door of Protesters and the West," *Guardian*, February 19, 2014, http://www.theguardian.com/world/2014/feb/19/russian-ukraine-putin-blames-west-protest.

94. Christopher Brennan, "Putin Sees No Political Future for Yanukovych," *Moscow Times*, March 5, 2014, http://www.themoscowtimes.com/news/article/putin-sees-no-political-future-for-yanukovych/495564.html.

95. Conversation with senior Russian political figure, May 22, 2014, Brussels.

96. BBC, "Ukraine: Transcript of Leaked Nuland-Pyatt Call," February 7, 2014, http://www.bbc.com/news/world-europe-26079957.

97. BBC, "Ukraine Crisis Timeline," http://www.bbc.com/news/world-middle-east-26248275; *Washington Post*, "Timeline: Key Events in Ukraine's Ongoing Crisis," http://www.washingtonpost.com/world/europe/timeline-key-events-in-ukraines-ongoing-crisis/2014/05/07/a15b84e6-d604-11e3-8a78-8fe50322a72c_story.html.

98. The International Republic institute, Public Opinion Survey, Residents of Ukraine August 27–September 9, 2013, http://www.iri.org/sites/default/files/IRI_Ukraine_August-September_2013_Edited%20Poll.pdf.

99. The International Republic institute, Public Opinion Survey, Residents of Ukraine April 3–12, 2014, http://www.iri.org/sites/default/files/2014%20April%2024%20Survey%20of%20Residents%20of%20Ukraine%2C%20April%203-12%2C%202014.pdf.

100. Boris Koloniskii, "Why Russians Back Putin on Ukraine," *New York Times*, March 11, 2014, http://www.nytimes.com/2014/03/12/opinion/why-russians-back-putin-on-ukraine.html.

101. Carol Matlack, "Why Putin's Ukrainian New Russia Could Be an Ungovernable Mess," *Bloomberg Businessweek*, May 5, 2014, http://www.businessweek.com/articles/2014-05-05/why-putins-ukrainian-new-russia-could-be-an-ungovernable-mess.

102. Anthony Faiola, "Ukrainian President Offers Rebels Major Concessions," *Washington Post*, September 15, 2014, http://www.washington-post.com/world/heavy-fighting-between-ukrainian-forces-and-pro-russian-rebels-over-the-weekend/2014/09/15/9f522a6c-1a27-4f3a-8c6a-5432c92911a3_story.html.

3   Impact of the Crisis on Russia

1. Zbigniew Brzezinski, *The Grand Chessboard: American Primacy and Its Geostrategic Imperatives* (New York: Basic Books, 1997).

2. "Iyuksliye reitingi odobrenia I doveriya," Levada Center, July 24, 2014, http://www.levada.ru/24-07-2014/iyulskie-reitingi-odobreniya-i-doveriya.

3. "Situatsiya na yug-vostoke Ukrainy," Levada Center, July 29, 2014, http://www.levada.ru/29-07-2014/situatsiya-na-yugo-vostoke-ukrainy.

4. "Reaktsiya Rossiyan na sanktsii," Levada Center, July 29, 2014, http://www.levada.ru/29-07-2014/reaktsiya-rossiyan-na-sanktsii.

5. Ariel Cohen and Helle Dale, "Russian Anti-Americanism: A Priority Target for U.S. Public Diplomacy," The Heritage Foundation Bac-

grounder 2373, February 24, 2010, http://www.heritage.org/research/
reports/2010/02/russian-anti-americanism-a-priority-target-for-us-public-
diplomacy.

6. Miriam Elder, "Vladimir Putin Accuses Hillary Clinton of Encourag-
ing Russian protests," *Guardian*, December 8, 2011, http://www.the-
guardian.com/world/2011/dec/08/vladimir-putin-hillary-clinton-
russia.

7. Lynn Berry and Vladimir Isachenkov, "A Tearful Putin Claims Election Victory," Associated Press, March 5, 2012, http://news.yahoo.com/
tearful-putin-claims-russian-election-victory-230110472.html.

8. "President orders limit on foreign ownership in Russian mass media,"
RT, October 15, 2014, http://rt.com/politics/196084-russia-mass-media-
foreign/.

9. "Vladimir Putin Held a Security Council Meeting on Countering
National Security Threats in the Information Sphere," Kremlin.ru, October 1, 2014, http://eng.kremlin.ru/transcripts/23029.

10. Charles Clover, "Russia in Grip of Clean-Living Orthodoxy," *Financial Times*, October 23, 2012, http://www.ft.com/intl/cms/s/0/487f
0600-1cf5-11e2-a17f-00144feabdc0.html#axzz3K0blfJO1.

11. "The Russian President Gave His Reasons for the Annexation of a
Region of Ukraine," *Prague Post*, March 18, 2014, http://praguepost.
com/eu-news/37854-full-text-of-putin-s-speech-on-crimea.

12. Aleksandr Baunov, "Novaya kontseptsia otechestva. Rossiya teper'
ne Yevropa," Slon.ru, April 24, 2014, http://slon.ru/world/kontseptsiya_
otechestva-1091580.xhtml.

13. Gabriela Baczynska, "Russia's Putin Tightens Grip on Elites with
Overseas Assets Ban," Reuters, August 29, 2013, http://www.reuters.
com/article/2013/08/29/russia-assets-idUSL6N0GS3U420130829.

14. Vladimir Ryzhkov, "Controlling Russians through Travel Bans,"
Moscow Times, May 26, 2014, http://www.themoscowtimes.com/opin-
ion/article/controlling-russians-through-travel-bans/500914.html.

15. "'Russia to develop own weapons manufacture'—Rogozin," *Russia Today*, August 24, 2012, http://rt.com/politics/rogozin-weapon-import-defense-485/.

16. "'Western Sanctions Will Only Strengthen Russian Industry'—Rogozin," *Russia Today*, March 13, 2014, http://rt.com/politics/rogozin-sanctions-boomerang-russian-582/comments/. "Russia Can Build Own Mistral Warships, Rogozin Says," *Moscow Times*, July 30, 2014, http://www.themoscowtimes.com/business/article/russia-can-build-own-mistral-warships-rogozin-says-/504343.html. "'Russian Defense Sector Should Rely on Domestic Technology'—Russian Official," RIA Novosti, April 4, 2014, http://en.ria.ru/military_news/20140404/189039840/Russian-Defense-Sector-Should-Rely-on-Domestic-Technology-.html.

17. Matthew Bodner, "Putin Urges Rapid Switch to Domestic Production in Defense Industry," *Moscow Times*, July 28, 2014, http://www.themoscowtimes.com/business/article/putin-urges-rapid-switch-to-domestic-production-in-defense-industry/504174.html.

18. Kathrin Hille, "Russian Looks for Economic Self-Reliance," *Financial Times*, April 22, 2014, http://www.ft.com/intl/cms/s/0/ee5d9120-ca2f-11e3-bb92-00144feabdc0.html#axzz39AShdj89.

19. "Puitn rasporyadilsya 'vernut' krupnyy bizness v Rossiyu," *Praim*, May 28, 2014, http://prime.ria.ru/Politics/20140528/785696980.html.

20. Kathrin Hille, "Russian Looks for Economic Self-Reliance," *Financial Times*, April 22, 2014. http://www.ft.com/intl/cms/s/0/ee5d9120-ca2f-11e3-bb92-00144feabdc0.html#axzz39AShdj89. "An Acronym with Capital," *Economist*, July 19, 2014, http://www.economist.com/news/finance-and-economics/21607851-setting-up-rivals-imf-and-world-bank-easier-running-them-acronym. "G7 Reported Freezing New World Bank Projects in Russia," *Russia Today*, August 1, 2014, http://rt.com/business/177384-g7-freeze-worldbank-russia/comments/page-2/.

21. "Joint Statement by Obama, Russian President Putin," The White House, June 18, 2012, http://translations.state.gov/st/english/text-trans/2012/06/201206187628.html#axzz39ElkD8RW.

22. Thomas Hirst, "The Russian Parliament Just Passed That Crazy Law Letting The Government Seize Foreign Assets," *Business Insider*, October 8,2014,http://www.businessinsider.com/russian-government-passed-law-allowing-government-to-seize-foreign-assets-2014-10.

23. Anastasia Bashkatova, "Rossiya-2015. Scenariy Khuzhe Nekuda," *Nezavisimaya Gazeta*, October 16, 2014, http://www.ng.ru/economics/2014-10-16/1_russia2015.html.

24. Kathrin Hille, "Russian Looks for Economic Self-Reliance," *Financial Times*, April 22, 2014, http://www.ft.com/intl/cms/s/0/ee5d9120-ca2f-11e3-bb92-00144feabdc0.html#axzz39AShdj89.

25. Boris Rumer, "The Search for Stability in Central Asia," in Boris Rumer, ed., *Central Asia: A Gathering Storm?* (Armonk, NY: M.E. Sharpe, 2002); Marlene Laruelle, *Russian Eurasianism: An Ideology of Empire*, (Woodrow Wilson Center Press and Johns Hopkins University Press, 2008).

26. Aleksandr I. Solzhenitsyn, *Letter to Soviet Leaders* (New York: Harper & Row, 1974).

27. Andreas Umland, "Who Is Aleksandr Dugin?" *Open Democracy*, September 26, 2008, https://www.opendemocracy.net/article/russia-theme/who-is-alexander-dugin. "Fascist Tendencies in Russian Higher Education: The Rise of Aleksandr Dugin and the Faculty of Sociology of Moscow State University," *Democratizatsiya*, Spring 2011. http://www.academia.edu/854121/Fascist_Tendencies_in_Russian_Higher_Education_The_Rise_of_Aleksandr_Dugin_and_the_Faculty_of_Sociology_of_Moscow_State_University. Dina Newman, "Russian Nationalist Thinker Dugin Sees War with Ukraine," BBC, July 9, 2014, http://www.bbc.com/news/world-europe-28229785.

28. Vladislav Inozemtsev, "Russkiy mir I protiv Russkogo mira II," *Vedomosti*, July 29, 2014, http://www.vedomosti.ru/opinion/news/29555761/russkij-mir-protiv-russkogo-mira.

29. Conversation with a senior Russian official, Moscow, July 18, 2014.

30. Anastasia Kashevarova, "Dmitriy Kiselev: 'Povedeniye Zapada granichit s shizofreniyey'," *Izvestiya*, April 4, 2014, http://izvestia.ru/news/568611.

31. "The Russian President Gave His Reasons for the Annexation of a Region of Ukraine," *Prague Post*, March 18, 2014, http://praguepost.com/eu-news/37854-full-text-of-putin-s-speech-on-crimea.

32. Conversation with a senior Kremlin official, Moscow, July 18, 2014.

33. Luke Harding and Matthew Weaver, "Barack Obama Calls for 'Reset' in US-Russia Relations," *Guardian*, July 7, 2009, http://www.theguardian.com/world/2009/jul/07/barack-obama-russia-moscow-speech.

34. "'Russia Was Prepared for Georgian Aggression'—Putin," *Russia Today*, August 8, 2012, http://rt.com/politics/putin-ossetia-war-plan-168/.

35. CIA World Factbook, https://www.cia.gov/library/publications/the-world-factbook/geos/kz.html.

36. Robert Coalson, "News Analysis: Armenian Choice Stirs Competition between Moscow, EU," RFE/RL, September 4, 2013, http://www.rferl.org/content/armenia-russia-customs-union-eu-analysys/25095948.html.

37. Joanna Lillis, "Kazakhstan: Debating the Fruits of the Customs Union," Eurasianet.org, October 11, 2013, http://www.eurasianet.org/node/67622.

38. "Kyrgyzstan Says Customs Union Member Next Year," RFE/RL, July 24, 2014, http://www.rferl.org/content/sarpashev-customs-union-russia-kazakhstan-belarus-road-map/25468399.html.

39. "Belarus', Kazakhstan Oppose Ukraine Import Restrictions, Report Says," *Moscow Times*, June 30, 2014, http://www.themoscowtimes.com/article/502719.html.

40. Alexander Panin, "For Russia, Eurasian Union Is about Politics, not Economy," *Moscow Times*, May 29, 2014, http://www.themos-

cowtimes.com/business/article/for-russia-eurasian-union-is-about-politics-not-economy/501126.html.

41. Rasul Zhunamly, "20 Voprosov Putinu iz Kazakhii," July 31, 2014, exclusive.kz. http://exclusive.kz/politika/25078.

42. Dmitrii Trenin, "China concentrates the mind," Moscow Carnegie Centre Briefing Papers, #5, 2001.

43. "Russia Signs 30-Year Gas Deal with China," BBC News, May 21, 2014, http://www.bbc.com/news/business-27503017.

44. Aleksandr Popov, "Mertvyy Vostok," July 12, 2009, Expertonline, http://expert.ru/expert/2012/27/mertvyij-vostok/. Sovet po Vneshney I Oboronnoy Politike (SVOP), "Novoye osvoyeniye Sibiri I Dal'nego Vostoka," 2001, http://svop.ru/public/pub2001/1288/. "Kitayskiy factor v novoy structure mezhdunarodnykh otnosheniy i startegiya Rossii," Nikitskiy klub, September 22, 2004, http://www.nikitskyclub.ru/article.php?idpublication=4&idissue=32.

45. Aleksandr Khramchikhin, "Kitayskaya ekspansiya neizbezhna," *Voyenno-Promyshlennyy Kur'yer*, September 4, 2013, http://vpk-news.ru/articles/17276. Aleksandr Khramchikhin, "Kitay gotovitsya k bol'shoy voyne," *Voyenno-Promushlennyy Kur'yer*, June 12, 2013, http://vpk-news.ru/articles/16297. Vladislav Shurygin, "Kitayskaya voyennaya ugroza," Vzglyad, May 15, 2012, http://vz.ru/opinions/2012/5/15/578969.html.

46. Yulia Latynina, "Kod Dostupa," *Ekho Moskvy*, May 24, 2014, http://echo.msk.ru/programs/code/1326254-echo/#element-text. The Editors, "In the Russia-China Gas Deal, Did Putin Win?" *Bloomberg View*, May 21, 2014, http://www.bloombergview.com/articles/2014-05-21/in-the-russia-china-gas-deal-did-putin-win. "Gazprom podpisal 30-letniy gazovyy kontrakt s Kitayem," Newsru.com, May 21, 2014, http://newsru.com/finance/21may2014/cnpcontract.html.

47. "Rising China, Sinking Russia," *Economist*, September 14, 2013. http://www.economist.com/news/asia/21586304-vast-region-chinas-economic-clout-more-match-russias-rising-china-sinking.

48. Max Strasser, "Ukraine: Why Is China Sitting on the Fence?" *Newsweek*, March 23, 2014, http://www.newsweek.com/ukraine-why-china-sitting-fence-232691.

49. Yu Bin, "Guns and Games of August: Tales of Two Strategic Partners," *Comparative Connections*, October 2008, http://csis.org/files/media/csis/pubs/0803qchina_russia.pdf.

50. William E.Odom, *The Collapse of the Soviet Military* (New Haven: Yale University Press, 2000). Anatol Lieven, *Chechnya: The Tombstone of Russian Power* (New Haven: Yale University Press, 1998).

51. "Putin's New Model Army," *Economist*, May 24, 2014, http://www.economist.com/news/europe/21602743-money-and-reform-have-given-russia-armed-forces-it-can-use-putins-new-model-army. Jakob Hendeskog and Carolina Vendil Pallin, eds., *Russian Military Capability in a 10-year Perspective-2013*, FOI-R-3734-SE, December 2013, http://www.foi.se/sv/Sok/Sammanfattningssida/?rNo=FOI-R--3734--SE.

52. "Minoborony utverzhdayet chto ne planirovalo zaklyuchat' novyye kntrakty po bespilotnikam s Izarailem," Newsru.com, August 6, 2014, http://newsru.com/russia/06aug2014/drones.html.

53. Johan Norberg and Fredrik Westerlund, "Russia and Ukraine: Military-Strategic Options and Possible Risks, for Moscow," FOI Memo 4904, RUFS Briefing No 22, April 2014, http://www.foi.se/Global/Vår%20kunskap/Säkerhetspolitiska%20studier/Ryssland/Briefings/RUFS%20Briefing%20No.22.pdf.

4   Europe and the Crisis

1. We speak here of war among the major powers within what is now the EU, not the eradication of war in Europe, which has not been achieved, as witness, for example, the conflicts between Turkey and Greece and the Soviet invasion of Hungary and Czechoslovakia.

2. European Commission, "Enlargement," (last updated March 17, 2014), http://ec.europa.eu/enlargement/.

3. European Union, External Action Service, "What is the European Neighborhood Policy?" n.d., http://eeas.europa.eu/enp/about-us/index_en.htm. (The ENP was succeeded in 2014 by the European Neighborhood Instrument.)

4. European Union, Eastern Partnership Community, "What is the Eastern Partnership?" July 1, 2014, http://www.easternpartnership.org/content/eastern-partnership-glance.

5. Stefan Meister and Marie-Lena May, "The EU's Eastern Partnership: A Misunderstood Offer of Cooperation," Deustche Gesellschaft fur Auswärtige Politik, *Standpunkt*, No. 7 (September 2009), 1-2.

6. Rosa Balfour, "Debating the Eastern Partnership: Perspectives from the European Union," *Internationale Politik und Gesselschaft*, Vol. 3 (July 2011), 33–36 is good on the diverging views within in the EU on EaP.

7. Details from "Russia Gives Ukraine Cheap Gas, $15 Billion," *Kyiv Post*, December 17, 2013, http://www.kyivpost.com/content/ukraine/russia-gives-ukraine-cheap-gas-15-billion-in-loans-333852.html.

8. "Ukraine's Bloodiest Day: Dozens Dead As Kiev Protestors Regain Territory From Police," *Guardian*, February 20, 2014, http://www.theguardian.com/world/2014/feb/20/ukraine-dead-protesters-police.

9. "Agreement On Settlement Of Crisis In Ukraine—Full Text," *Guardian*, February 21, 2014.

10. See, for example, Paweł Dariusz Wiśniewski, *The Eastern Partnership: It's High Time to Start a Real "Partnership'"*(Moscow: Carnegie Moscow Center, 2013), 14; "The World from Berlin: The EU's Eastern 'Sphere of Influence'," *Spiegel Online International*, May 6, 2009, http://www.spiegel.de/international/europe/the-world-from-berlin-the-eu-s-eastern-sphere-of-influence-a-623163.html; Meister and Way, "The EU's Eastern Partnership," 2; "EU's New Eastern Partnership Draws Ire from Russia," *European Dialogue*, n.d., http://www.eurodialogue.eu/668.

11. Wiśniewski, *Eastern Partnership*, 14; Jean Park, "The European Union's Eastern Partnership," Council on Foreign Relations, *Background-*

ers, March 14, 2014, http://www.cfr.org/europe/european-unions-eastern-partnership/p32577.

12. Meister and Way, "The EU's Eastern Partnership," 4. We should stress that Meister and Way reject the idea of a Russian sphere of influence in the post-Soviet states.

13. See "The EU's Association Agreements with Georgia, the Republic of Moldova, and Ukraine," European Commission, Memo 14/140, June 23, 2014, http://europa.eu/rapid/press-release_MEMO-14-430_en.htm for the pre-signature announcement by the EU.

14. For an extended discussion based on interviews in Kyiv and Donetsk with senior Ukrainian leaders and business people, see Rajan Menon, *The Two Ukraines*, Foreign Policy Program, German Marshall Fund, July 2011, http://www.gmfus.org/galleries/ct_publication_attachments/Menon_TwoUkraines_Jul11.pdf.

15. "Ukraine's Biggest Trade Partners: Countries," Bloomberg.com, http://www.bloomberg.com/visual-data/best-and-worst/ukraines-biggest-trading-partners-countries.

16. "Ukraine-EU Trade A Big Threat to Russia's Economy," BBC News, November 26, 2013, http://www.bbc.com/news/world-europe-25108022.

17. For details, see Česlovas Iškaukus, "The Third Energy Package: Dispute Between Russia and the EU," *European Dialogue*, June 4, 2011, http://www.eurodialogue.eu/Third-Energy-Package-dispute-between-Russia-and-the-EU; "Russia Sues EU Over Its 'Third Energy Package'," *Voice of Russia*, May 1, 2014, http://voiceofrussia.com/news/2014_05_01/Russia-sues-EU-over-its-Third-Energy-Package-4716/; World Trade Organization, "Russia Files Dispute Against EU Over Regulations in the Energy Sector," April 30, 2014, http://www.wto.org/english/news_e/news14_e/ds476rfc_30apr14_e.htm.

18. EU, Energy Community, *News Details*, July 28, 2014, http://www.energy-community.org/portal/page/portal/ENC_HOME/NEWS/News_Details?p_new_id=9401.

19. NATO, "NATO-EU: A Strategic Partnership," n.d., http://www.nato.int/cps/en/natolive/topics_49217.htm.

20. NATO, "Bucharest Summit Declaration," April 3, 2008, http://www.nato.int/cps/en/natolive/official_texts_8443.htm.

21. See Aleksandr Dugin, "Open Letter to the American People on Ukraine," March 8, 2014, http://openrevolt.info/2014/03/08/alexander-dugin-letter-to-the-american-people-on-ukraine/; "Foes of Russia in Ukraine Crave Rupture of Ties," *New York Times,* March 15, 2014.

22. Anton Barbarshin and Hannah Thoburn, "Putin's Brain: Alexander Dugin and The Philosophy Behind Putin's Invasion of Crimea," *Foreign Affairs*, March 31, 2014, http://www.foreignaffairs.com/articles/141080/anton-barbashin-and-hannah-thoburn/putins-brain; Paul Goble, "Window on Eurasia: Is the Izborsky Club Losing Its Clout?", July 7, 2014, http://windowoneurasia2.blogspot.com/2014/07/window-on-eurasia-is-izborsky-club.html; Wayne Allensworth, "Dugin and the Eurasian Controversy: Is Eurasianism 'Patriotic'?" in Marlene Laruelle, ed., *Russian Nationalism and the National Reassertion of Russia* (New York: Routledge, 2009), 104–110; Michael Khodarkovsky, "Glory to the 'Russian World'," *New York Times*, October 13, 2014.

23. "Russia Claims Its Sphere of Influence in the World," *New York Times*, August 31, 2008.

24. "Russia Suspended From the G8 But Not Expelled," *Financial Times,* March 24, 2014.

25. France TV24, "World Leaders Arrive in France for D-Day Celebrations," June 6, 2014, http://www.france24.com/en/20140605-word-leaders-flock-france-d-day-celebrations-70-years/; "Western Leaders Line Up to Meet Putin in France During D-Day Celebrations," *Pravda* (in English), June 6, 2014, http://english.pravda.ru/world/europe/06-06-2014/127747-putin_normandy-0/. Putin and Obama did meet informally following the D-Day luncheon. "Awkward Diplomacy As Leaders Gather," *New York Times*, June 6, 2014.

26. "France Hosts D-Day Celebrations Attended By World Leaders," RIA Novosti, May 6, 2014, http://en.ria.ru/world/20140606/190385109/

France-Hosts-D-Day-Celebrations-Attended-by-World-Leaders.html; "Harper, Obama Opposed Meetings With Putin But Urged Tough Messages," *Huffington Post,* June 5, 2014, http://www.huffingtonpost. ca/2014/06/05/stephen-harper-vladimir-putin-d-day_n_5450322.html; "Harper, Obama Opposed G7 Meeting With Putin," Canadian Broadcasting Corporation, June 5, 2014, http://www.cbc.ca/m/touch/news/ story/1.2666102.

27. US Census Bureau, Foreign Trade, "Trade in Goods With Russia," https://www.census.gov/foreign-trade/balance/c4621.htm#202.

28 European Commission, "Russia: Main Indicators," http://trade. ec.europa.eu/doclib/docs/2006/september/tradoc_111720.pdf. The EU trade data are in provided in Euros and we have converted them to US dollars using the August 18, 2014, exchange rate of 1: 1.34 in favor of the Euro. See also BBC News, "Russia's Trade Ties With Europe," March 14, 2014, http://www.bbc.com/news/world-europe-26436291.

29. World Bank, "Merchandise Trade (%GDP)," http://data.worldbank. org/indicator/TG.VAL.TOTL.GD.ZS.

30. Permanent Mission of the Russian Federation to the European Union, "Trade," http://www.russianmission.eu/en/trade. The figure is for 2012. Other sources estimate the proportion, also for 2012, at 41 percent: "Russia's Trade Ties With Europe," BBC News, March 4, 2014, http://www.bbc.com/news/world-europe-26436291.

31. European Union, Directorate General of Trade, "Russia: Main Indicators" n.d.; European Commission, Directorate-General for Trade, trade.ec.europa.eu/doclib/html/111720.htm; "European Union, Trade With Russia," April 16, 2014, trade.ec.europa.eu/doclib/html/113440. htm; On Russia's role in German, French, Italian, and British trade, see Statistisches Bundesamt, *Foreign Trade: Ranking of Germany's Trading Partners in Foreign Trade,* July 24, 2014; Alpha Bank, "International Trade, France: Trade Profile," http://www.alphainternationaltrade.com/ en/choose-your-markets/country-profiles/france/trade-profile#classification_by_country; *ING Bank, Developments In Global Trade from 1995 to 2017, Italy,* November 23, 2012, http://www.ingcb. com/media/231170/italy.pdf; "UK Export and Import in 2011: Top

Products and Trading Partners," *Guardian*, posted January 10, 2012, http://www.theguardian.com/news/datablog/2010/feb/24/uk-trade-exports-imports.

32. "Euro-Zone Economy Slips in the First Quarter as German GDP Slips," *Wall Street Journal*, August 14, 2014, http://online.wsj.com/articles/french-gdp-fails-to-grow-in-second-quarter-1407994573.

33. "German GDP Shrinking Signals Fading Euro-Area Powerhouse," Bloomberg News, September 1, 2014, http://www.bloomberg.com/news/2014-09-01/german-gdp-shrinking-signals-fading-euro-area-powerhouse.html.

34. Data in European Commission, Eurostat, "Unemployment Statistics," (data up to June 2014), http://epp.eurostat.ec.europa.eu/statistics_explained/index.php/Unemployment_statistics#Unemployment_trends.

35. For details, see "Crimea Crisis Has Little Impact Thus Far on Russian Oil Deals," *New York Times,* March 28, 2014; "Russia Sanctions Threaten to Blow Euro Zone Off Course," Reuters, July 29, 2014, http://www.reuters.com/article/2014/07/29/ukraine-crisis-eurozone-idUSL6N0Q421J20140729;http://www.eon-russia.ru/en/investments/; "Airbus in Russia," airbus.com, n.d., http://www.airbus.com/company/worldwide-presence/airbus-in-russia/; "Putin Strikes Back Against Sanctions With Food Import Bans," *Moscow Times*, August 6, 2014, http://www.themoscowtimes.com/business/article/putin-orders-agricultural-import-bans-on-countries-that-sanctioned-russia/504675.html; "Russia Sanctions Show Putin's 'Short-Sighted Desperation,' Canada Says," Canadian Broadcasting Corporation, August 7, 2014, http://www.cbc.ca/news/world/russia-sanctions-show-putin-s-short-sighted-desperation-canada-says-1.2729821; "Who Is Hit Hardest By Russia's Trade Ban?," *Russia Today*, August 8, 2014, http://rt.com/business/178888-russia-trade-ban-who-hurts/.

36. US Energy Information Administration, "US Natural Gas Imports By Country" (release date: July 31, 2014), http://www.eia.gov/dnav/ng/ng_move_impc_s1_a.htm.

37. Bloomberg News, "Years Needed For LNG Exports to Blunt Russia Energy Sales," Bloomberg.com, March 7, 2014, http://www.bloomberg.com/news/2014-03-07/years-needed-for-lng-exports-to-blunt-russia-energy-sales.html; Steve Mufson, "Can US Natural Gas Rescue Russia from Ukraine?" *Washington Post*, March 25, 2014; Jay Zawatsky, "LNG Won't Save Europe," *National Interest* (online), April 23, 2014, http://nationalinterest.org/feature/lng-wont-save-europe-10295.

38. Data from US Energy Information Administration, "Today in Energy," July 23, 2014, http://www.eia.gov/todayinenergy/detail.cfm?id=17231.

39. See, for example, "Despite Pressure France Won't Cancel Warship Deal with Russia," Reuters, May 12, 2014, http://www.reuters.com/article/2014/05/12/us-france-russia-mistral-idUSBREA4B08V20140512; "MH17 Plane Crash: EU to Widen Russia Sanctions," July 22, 2014, http://www.bbc.com/news/uk-28415248; "'Hypocrites!': Hollande Hits back at Cameron Attacking France Selling Warships to Russia While Oligarchs Seek Refuge in London," *Daily Mail*, July 22, 2014; http://www.dailymail.co.uk/news/article-2701158/Cameron-tells-EU-countries-needs-hit-sanctions-against-Russia-banking-energy-defence.html.

40. On EU and US Sanctions, see Baker McKenzie, "Sanctions Update," http://www.bakermckenzie.com/sanctionsnews/.

41. "French Mistral Sale Strategy: Buy Time to Maneuver," *Defense News*, September 6, 2014, http://www.defensenews.com/article/20140906/DEFREG01/309060019/French-Mistral-Sale-Strategy-Buy-Time-Maneuver.

42. European Council, "Further Economic Measures on Russia," September 11, 2014, http://www.european-council.europa.eu/home-page/highlights/further-economic-sanctions-on-russia?lang=en.

43. For a list of EU sanctions through September 2014, see "Further Economic Measures on Russia."

44. "In Reprisal, Russia Imposes Trade Sanctions On the West," *New York Times*, August 7, 2014. Some sources, citing US government data, report that agricultural sales to Russia totaled $1.2 billion but perhaps

that figures excludes some foodstuffs counted in the $1.6 billion figure. "Russia Bans Food Imports In Retaliation for Western Sanctions," *Wall Street Journal,* August 7, 2014, http://online.wsj.com/articles/russia-bans-food-imports-in-retaliation-to-western-sanctions-1407403035. For the list of banned food products, see "Russia Responds to Sanctions By Banning Western Food Imports," *Guardian*, August 7, 2014. On the relative cost to US versus Europe, see the analysis and the sources sited in Rajan Menon, "A Game of Russian Roulette? The West's Dangerous Sanctions Play Against Russia," *National Interest* (online), August 14, 2014, http://nationalinterest.org/feature/game-russian-roulette-the-wests-dangerous-sanctions-play-11075.

45. "Russia Cuts Gas to Ukraine While Maintaining Flows to Europe," Bloomberg News, June 16, 2014, http://www.bloomberg.com/news/2014-06-16/ukraine-faces-russian-gas-cutoff-as-payment-talks-fail.html; "Russia Tells Ukraine to Pay $3.9 Billion to Resume Gas Supplies, *Wall Street Journal,* September 30, 2014, http://online.wsj.com/articles/russia-tells-ukraine-to-pay-3-9-billion-to-resume-gas-supplies-1412071535.

46. "Ukraine Says Russia Ready to Compromise on Gas Price with Ukraine," *Moscow Times*, August 20, 2014, http://www.themoscowtimes.com/business/article/ukraine-says-ready-to-compromise-on-gas-price-with-russia/505455.html.

47. "Russia Tightens Gas Supplies to Poland," *Financial Times*, September 10, 2014; "Russia Halves Natural Gas Supplies to Slovakia," *Wall Street Journal*, October 1, 2014, http://online.wsj.com/articles/russia-halves-natural-gas-supplies-to-slovakia-1412177795.

48. For the growth rate see World Bank, "Russia's Monthly Economic Developments," September 16, 2014, http://www.worldbank.org/en/country/russia/brief/monthly-economic-developments. On capital flight, see "ECB: Capital Flight from Russia Has Hit $220 Billion," *Telegraph*, May 8, 2014, http://www.telegraph.co.uk/finance/financialcrisis/10817511/ECB-capital-flight-from-Russia-has-hit-220bn.html and "Russia See Further Rise in Capital Flight, *Wall Street Journal*, July 9, 2014, http://online.wsj.com/articles/russia-sees-further-rise-in-capital-

flight-1404918861; "Hungary Halts Flow of Gas to Ukraine," *Financial Times*, September 26, 2014, http://www.ft.com/cms/s/0/7c5d2bf0-4552-11e4-ab86-00144feabdc0.html#axzz3GPhlGy81.

49. Data on public debt from Central Intelligence Agency, Word Factbook, "Russia," https://www.cia.gov/library/publications/the-world-factbook/geos/rs.html; Data on external debt from Bank of Russia, "External Debt of the Russian Federation" (Updated July 25, 2014), http://www.cbr.ru/eng/statistics/print.aspx?file=credit_statistics/debt_an_det_new_e.htm&pid=svs&sid=itm_272 and "External Debt (Percentage of GDP)—By Country," MacroeconomyMeter.com, http://meco meter.com/topic/external-debt-percentage-of-gdp/.

50. On the importance states attach to honor, pride, and standing, see Richard Ned Lebow, *Why Nations Fight: Past and Future Motives for War* (Cambridge: Cambridge University Press, 2010).

51. "Why Nothing Will Dent Vladimir Putin's Popularity at Home," *Guardian*, July 31, 2014; Armin Rosen, "Sanctions Have Little Effect on Putin's Incredible Popularity at Home," *Business Insider*, July 29, 2014, http://www.businessinsider.com/putins-position-within-russia-seems-secure-2014-7; "As Sanctions Pile Up Russians' Alarm Grows Over Putin's Tactics," *New York Times*, July 29, 2014; Sam Greene and Graeme Robertson, "Explaining Putin's Popularity: Rallying Around the Russian Flag," *Washington Post*, September 9, 2014, http://www.washingtonpost.com/blogs/monkey-cage/wp/2014/09/09/explaining-putins-popularity-rallying-round-the-russian-flag/.

52. Leonid Bershidsky, "Eastern Europe: Don't Sanction Putin," *Bloomberg View*, August 15, 2014, http://www.bloombergview.com/articles/2014-08-15/eastern-europe-don-t-sanction-putin; "Czechs Opposes Broad Sanctions, See New Iron Curtain," Reuters, July 30, 2014, http://www.reuters.com/article/2014/07/30/us-ukraine-crisis-czech-idUSKBN0FZ17Y20140730.

53. This section draws on Rajan Menon, "Why The Ukraine Crisis Won't Save NATO," *National Interest* (online), April 1, 2014, http://nationalinterest.org/commentary/why-the-ukraine-crisis-wont-save-nato-10165.

54. For an early and acute analysis, see Michael Mandelbaum, *The Dawn of Peace in Europe* (New York: Twentieth Century Fund Press, 1996), Chs. 1–3. Also see Rajan Menon, *The End of Alliances* (New York: Oxford University Press, 2007), Ch. 2.

55. Johanna Granville, "After Kosovo: The Impact of NATO Expansion on Political Parties, *Demokratizatsiya*, Vol. 8 No.1 (Winter 2000), esp. 37–40; J.L. Black, "Russia and NATO Expansion: Red-Lining the Baltic States," *International Journal*, Vol. 54, No. 2 (Spring, 1999), 249-266; Eric Shiraev and Olga Makhovskaya, "From the Cold War to Lukewarm Peace: Russian Views of September 11 and Beyond," in David Faber, ed., *What They Think of US: International Perceptions of the United States Since 9/11* (Princeton: Princeton University Press, 2007), 99–102.

56. There has been a long and heated debate in the United States, and the West more generally, over the need for, and wisdom of, NATO expansion. It is incidental to our purpose in this book and thus will not be reprised. But for a recent account that revisits the controversy, see Michael E. Brown, "NATO's Biggest Mistake," *Foreign Affairs,* May 5, 2014, http://www.foreignaffairs.com/articles/138432/michael-e-brown/natos-biggest-mistake.

57. We owe this point to Thomas Graham.

58. Mark Kramer, "The Myth Of A No-NATO-Enlargement Pledge to Russia," *Washington Quarterly*, Vol. 32, No. 2 (April 2009), 39–61.

59. NATO, "NATO Enlargement," n.d., http://www.nato.int/cps/en/natolive/topics_49212.htm.

60. Lugar recalled this in his September 20, 2009 speech on NATO at the Atlantic Council. For the transcript, see "Transcript: Senator Lugar—Congressional Perspective on the Future of NATO," http://www.atlanticcouncil.org/news/transcripts/transcript-senator-lugar-congressional-perspective-on-the-future-of-nato.

61. "NATO After Libya: A Troubling Victory," *Economist*, September 3, 2011; Ellen Hallams and Benjamin Scheerer, "Toward A Post-American Alliance? NATO Burden Sharing After Libya," *International Affairs*, Vol. 88, No. 2 (2012), 313–327.

62. See Rajan Menon, "NATO, RIP," *American Interest,* Vol. 4, No. 2 (November/December 2008), pp. 52-59.

63. "Russia's Moves in Ukraine Are 'Wake Up' Call, NATO's Rasmussen Says in Speech," *Washington Post,* March 19, 2014; NATO, "North Atlantic Council Statement on the Situation in Ukraine," March 2, 2014; On speeches by official from NATO states, see, for example, closing keynote speech by Vice President Joe Biden at the Atlantic Council conference on "NATO Whole and Free," April 30, 2014, http://www.atlanticcouncil.org/news/transcripts/remarks-by-vice-president-joe-biden-at-the-atlantic-council-s-toward-a-europe-whole-and-free-conference;   Speech by Norwegian Defense Minister Eine Eriksen Søreide, at Chatham House, April 29, 2014, Norway, Ministry of Defense, http://www.regjeringen.no/nb/dep/fd/aktuelt/taler_artikler/ministeren/taler-og-artikler-av-forsvarsminister-in/2014/Speech-at-Chatham-House-London-Norway-NATO-and-the-Crisis-in-Ukraine.html?id=758246.

64. For the text, see NATO, "The North Atlantic Treaty," http://www.nato.int/cps/en/natolive/official_texts_17120.htm.

65. "Obama Rules Out Military Force Over Ukraine," *New York Times,* March 20, 2014, http://www.nytimes.com/2014/03/21/world/europe/obama-ukraine.html?_r=0.

66. See CNN reporter Candy Crowley's March 16, 2014 interview with McCain: http://transcripts.cnn.com/TRANSCRIPTS/1403/16/sotu.01.html.

67. "Concerns About Russia Rise, But Just a Quarter Call Moscow and Adversary: Public Remains Wary About US Involvement in Ukraine," Pew Research Center for People and the Press, March 25, 2014, http://www.people-press.org/2014/03/25/concerns-about-russia-rise-but-just-a-quarter-call-moscow-an-adversary/; "Politico Poll: Stay Out of Ukraine, Middle East," Politico.com, July 21, 2014 (updated July 22, 2014), http://www.politico.com/story/2014/07/politico-poll-ukraine-middle-east-109155.html.

68. Peter Moore, "Public Against Getting Involved in Ukraine, Even After MH17," YouGov.com, July 22, 2014, https://today.yougov.com/news/2014/07/22/public-against-us-getting-involved-ukraine/

69. "Merkel Sceptical of NATO Deployments in Eastern Europe," EurActiv.com, March 7, 2014, http://www.euractiv.com/sections/europes-east/merkel-sceptical-nato-deployments-eastern-europe-303276; "German Leader Emerges As Key Figure in Ukraine Talks," *New York Times,* August 19, 2014; "Ukraine Crisis: Poland Asks NATO To Station 10,000 Troops On Its Territory," *Daily Telegraph*, April 1, 2014, http://www.telegraph.co.uk/news/worldnews/europe/ukraine/10737838/Ukraine-crisis-Poland-asks-Nato-to-station-10000-troops-on-its-territory.html.

70. Mark Thompson, "NATO's Back in Business, Thanks to Ukraine," *Time*, April 16, 2014.

71. "Unprotected in the East" NATO Appears Toothless in Ukraine Crisis," *Der Spiegel,* May 19, 2014, http://www.spiegel.de/international/germany/ukraine-crisis-shows-up-cracks-in-nato-a-970248.html.

72. "Merkel Says She's Against Arming Ukraine, But Sanctions Are Coming," *Kyiv Post*, August 31, 2014, http://www.kyivpost.com/content/ukraine/merkel-says-shes-against-arming-ukraine-but-says-sanctions-are-coming-362751.html; "Romania Calls On EU, NATO To Arm Ukraine" *GlobalPost*, August 29, 2014, http://www.globalpost.com/dispatch/news/afp/140829/romania-calls-eu-nato-arm-ukraine;   "Ukraine Crisis: Russia In 'A State of War'" With Our Continent, European Leaders Warn, *Independent,* August 31, 2014, http://www.independent.co.uk/news/world/europe/ukraine-crisis-eu-summit-seeks-to-show-it-backs-kiev-9701806.html: "Lithuania Calls on EU to Arm Ukraine Amid Crisis," *Baltic Times,* September 1, 2014, http://www.baltictimes.com/news/articles/35442/#.VDVXjyldUjE; "Polish Defense Minister: Poland is Ready to Sell Arms to Ukraine," *Moscow Times,* September 22, 2014, http://www.themoscowtimes.com/advertorials/news/Polish-Defense-Minister-Poland-Is-Ready-to-Sell-Arms-to-Ukraine/; "Romania Calls on EU, NATO to Arm Ukraine," *Focus*, August 29, 2014.

73. European Commission, Eurostat, "The EU in the World—Economy and Finance," http://epp.eurostat.ec.europa.eu/statistics_explained/index.php/The_EU_in_the_world_-_economy_and_finance.

74. NATO, Public Diplomacy Division, "Financial and Economic Data Relating to NATO Defence," February 24, 2014, http://www.nato.int/nato_static/assets/pdf/pdf_topics/20140224_140224-PR2014-028-Defence-exp.pdf.

75. McKinsey and Company, *The Future of European Defense: Tackling the Productivity Challenge* (2013); John Dowdy, Gundbert Scherf, and Wolff van Sintern, "Enlisting Productivity to Reinforce European Defense," McKinsey and Company, Insights and Publications, August 2013, http://www.mckinsey.com/insights/public_sector/enlisting_productivity_to_reinforce_european_defense.

76. See the list of opinion polls in Campaign for America's Future, "The American Majority Project Polling," http://ourfuture.org/report/american-majority-project-polling;" Among American Voters, Poll Finds Unprecedented Anxiety About Jobs, Economy," *Washington Post*, November 25, 2013; "Most Americans Favor Cuts Overall—But Not to Military," ABC News/Washington Post Poll, 2013, http://www.langerresearch.com/uploads/1144a13TheSequester.pdf; R. Jeffrey Smith, "Public Overwhelmingly Supports Large Defense Cuts," Center for Public Integrity, May 10, 2012 (updated May 19, 2014), http://www.publicintegrity.org/2012/05/10/8856/public-overwhelmingly-supports-large-defense-spending-cuts; John T. Bennett, "Survey: Majority of Voters Favor Defense Cuts," *US News & World Report*, July 16, 2012, http://www.usnews.com/news/blogs/dotmil/2012/07/16/survey-majority-of-voters-favor-defense-cuts; Amanda Ruggeri, "Poll: Americans Strongly Back Spending on Infrastructure," *US New & World Report*, January 8, 2009, http://www.usnews.com/news/stimulus/articles/2009/01/08/poll-americans-strongly-back-increase-in-infrastructurespending.

77. See the details (in the report with a somewhat misleading title), Pew Research Center, Fact Tank, April 1, 2014, "Americans Disengaged, Feeling Less Respected, But Still See US as World Military Superpower," http://www.pewresearch.org/fact-tank/2014/04/01/americans-disen-

gaged-feeling-less-respected-but-still-see-u-s-as-worlds-military-super-power/; "Politico Poll: Stay Out of Ukraine, Middle East." The second poll, which was not limited to Ukraine and the Middle East, showed a wider opposition to increased military involvement abroad.

5   Ukraine's Prospects

1. Graham Stack, "Splits in Ukraine's pro-EU camp emerge over Poroshenko plan for East Ukraine," *Business New Europe*, September 16, 2014, http://www.bne.eu/content/story/splits-ukraines-pro-eu-camp-emerge-over-poroshenko-plan-east-ukraine.

2. Dmitry Zaks, "Ukraine could sack up to million officials with ties to Russian past," *AFP*, October 9, 2014, http://news.yahoo.com/ukraine-could-sack-million-officials-ties-russian-past-231947924.html.

3. Sergii Leshchenko, "Ukraine's Oligarchs Are still Calling the Shots," *Foreign Policy*, August 14, 2014, http://www.foreignpolicy.com/articles/2014/08/14/ukraines_oligarchs_are_still_calling_the_shots_0. Philip Shishkin, "Ukraine Taps Volunteers Fueled by Anger, Bravado," *Wall Street Journal*, August 15, 2014, http://www.foreignpolicy.com/articles/2014/08/14/ukraines_oligarchs_are_still_calling_the_shots_0.

4. Leonid Bershidskiy, "Ukraine's Revolutionaries Surrender to Corruption," *Bloomberg View*, August 18, 2014, http://www.bloombergview.com/articles/2014-08-18/ukraine-s-revolutionaries-surrender-to-corruption.

5. International Monetary Fund, "Ukraine: First Review Under Stand-by Arrangement," September 2014, http://www.imf.org/external/pubs/ft/scr/2014/cr14263.pdf.

6. Sandrine Rastello, "Ukraine Gets IMF Approval for $17 Billion Loan Amid Unrest," *Bloomberg*, April 30, 2014, http://www.bloomberg.com/news/2014-04-30/ukraine-gets-imf-approval-for-17-billion-loan-amid-unrest.html.

7. Carol J. Williams, "Ukraine Needs $35 Nillion in Aid to Avert Default, Interim Leaders Say," *Los Angeles Times*, February 24, 2014, http://www.

latimes.com/world/worldnow/la-fg-wn-ukraine-aid-default-20140224-story.html.

8. Daryna Krasnolutska, "IMF says Ukraine May Need \$19 Billion More Aid Amid War," *Bloomberg*, September 2, 2014, http://www.bloomberg.com/news/2014-09-02/imf-says-ukraine-may-need-19-billion-more-aid-amid-war.html.

9. Kathleen Holzwart Sprehe, "Ukraine Says 'No' to NATO," Pew Research Global Attitudes Project, March 29, 2010, http://www.pew-global.org/2010/03/29/ukraine-says-no-to-nato/.

10. Julia Ray and Neli Esipova, "Before Crisis, Ukrainians More Likely to See NATO as a Threat," *Gallup World*, March 14, 2014, http://www.gallup.com/poll/167927/crisis-ukrainians-likely-nato-threat.aspx.

11. Carol J. Williams, "Russian Aggression Driving Ukrainians toward EU, NATO, Poll Finds," *Los Angeles Times*, May 14, 2014, http://www.latimes.com/world/europe/la-fg-ukraine-russia-eu-nato-20140514-story.html.

12. Neil McFarquhar, "Gazprom Cuts Russia's Natural Gas Supply to Ukraine," *New York Times*, June 16, 2014, http://www.nytimes.com/2014/06/17/world/europe/russia-gazprom-increases-pressure-on-ukraine-in-gas-dispute.html.

13. Andrew Heavens, "EU Pays Out First Loan Tranche to Ukraine," Reuters, May 20, 2014, http://www.reuters.com/article/2014/05/20/us-ukraine-crisis-loan-idUSBREA4J0DT20140520.

14. Judy Dempsey, "After the Sanctions, a Strategy for the East," *Strategic Europe*, August 18, 2014, http://m.ceip.org/brussels/strategiceurope/?fa=56398.

6 Conclusion

1. Ronald Asmus, Richard Kugler, Stephen Larrabee, "Building A New NATO," *Foreign Affairs*, September–October 1993, http://www.foreignaffairs.com/articles/49201/ronald-d-asmus-richard-l-kugler-f-stephen-larrabee/building-a-new-nato.

Index

Note: Page numbers in italics indicate graphics.

About the Authors

Rajan Menon is the Anne and Bernard Spitzer Professor of Political Science at the Powell School, City College of New York/City University of New York, and Senior Research Scholar at the Saltzman Institute of War and Peace Studies, Columbia University. The author, most recently, of *The End of Alliances*, he is completing a book on humanitarian intervention and is a regular contributor to nationalinterest.org.

Eugene Rumer is a Senior Associate and Director of the Russia and Eurasia Program at the Carnegie Endowment for International Peace.

Boston Review Books

Boston Review Books is an imprint of *Boston Review*, a bimonthly magazine of ideas. The book series, like the magazine, covers a lot of ground. But a few premises tie it all together: that democracy depends on public discussion; that sometimes understanding means going deep; that vast inequalities are unjust; and that human imagination breaks free from neat political categories. Visit bostonreview.net for more information.

The End of the Wild   STEPHEN M. MEYER

God and the Welfare State   LEW DALY

Making Aid Work   ABHIJIT VINAYAK BANERJEE

The Story of Cruel and Unusual   COLIN DAYAN

Movies and the Moral Adventure of Life   ALAN A. STONE

The Road to Democracy in Iran   AKBAR GANJI

Why Nuclear Disarmament Matters   HANS BLIX

Race, Incarceration, and American Values   GLENN C. LOURY

The Men in My Life   VIVIAN GORNICK

Africa's Turn?   EDWARD MIGUEL

Inventing American History   WILLIAM HOGELAND

After America's Midlife Crisis   MICHAEL GECAN

Why We Cooperate   MICHAEL TOMASELLO

Taking Economics Seriously   DEAN BAKER

Rule of Law, Misrule of Men   ELAINE SCARRY

Immigrants and the Right to Stay   JOSEPH H. CARENS